PLAIN AND FANCY

Plain and Fancy

A MUSICAL COMEDY

by

Joseph Stein *and* **Will Glickman**

with lyrics by ARNOLD B. HORWITT

and music by ALBERT HAGUE

RANDOM HOUSE, NEW YORK

PLAIN AND FANCY *was first presented by Richard Kollmar and James W. Gardiner, in association with Yvette Schumer, at the Mark Hellinger Theatre, New York City, on January 27, 1955, with the following cast:*

(In order of appearance)

RUTH WINTERS	Shirl Conway
DAN KING	Richard Derr
A MAN	John Dennis
ANOTHER MAN	Chris Robinson
KATIE YODER	Gloria Marlowe
PAPA YODER	Stefan Schnabel
ISAAC MILLER	Sammy Smith
EMMA MILLER	Nancy Andrews
EZRA REBER	Douglas Fletcher Rodgers
HILDA MILLER	Barbara Cook
A YOUNG MILLER	Scotty Engel
ANOTHER YOUNG MILLER	Elaine Lynn
PETER REBER	David Daniels
RACHEL	Ethel May Cody
SAMUEL ZOOK	Daniel Nagrin
LEVI STOLZFUSS	William Weslow
JACOB YODER	Will Able
SAMUEL LAPP	Chris Robinson
ABNER ZOOK	Edgar Thompson
IKE PILERSHEIM	James S. Moore
MOSES ZOOK	John Dennis
ABNER ZOOK	Tim Worthington
AN AMISH MAN	Herbert Surface

v

PLAIN AND FANCY

ANOTHER AMISH MAN   Robert Lindgren
BESSIE   Faith Daltry
SARAH   Renee Orin
ESTHER   Sybil Lamb
REBECCA   Betty McGuire
MARY   Muriel Shaw
STATE TROOPER   Ray Hyson

Dancers: Sara Aman, Imelda DeMartin, Ina Hahn, Marcia Howard, Lucia Lambert, Joan Darby, Ann Needham, Tao Strong, Beryl Towbin, Saint Amant, Crandall Diehl, Ronnie Lee, Robert Lindgren, James S. Moore, Philip Nasta, Robert St. Clair, William Weslow, David Wood.

Singers: Marilyn Bradley, Faith Daltry, Janet Hayes, Sybil Lamb, Renee Orin, Betty McGuire, Muriel Shaw, Betty Zollinger, Ray Hyson, Jack Irwin, Robert Kole, Chris Robinson, John Dennis, Herbert Surface, Edgar F. Thompson, Tim Worthington, Paul Brown, Jim Schlader.

Production directed by Morton Da Costa

Dances and musical numbers staged by Helen Tamiris

Sets and costumes designed by Raoul Pene Dubois

Lighting by Peggy Clark

Orchestrations by Philip J. Lang

Vocal arrangements by Crane Calder

Orchestra and chorus directed by Franz Allers

SCENES

The entire action takes place in and around Bird-in-Hand, a town in the Amish country of Pennsylvania.

Time: The present

ACT ONE

ACT TWO

MUSICAL NUMBERS

ACT ONE

You Can't Miss It	Dan King, Ruth Winters and Ensemble
It Wonders Me	Katie Yoder
Plenty of Pennsylvania	Emma Miller, Ezra Reber, Young Miller and Ensemble
Young and Foolish	Peter Reber
Why Not Katie?	Ezra Reber and the Men
Young and Foolish (Reprise)	Katie Yoder, Peter Reber
By Lantern Light	Danced by Samuel Zook and others
It's a Helluva Way to Run a Love Affair	Ruth Winters
This Is All Very New to Me	Sung and danced by Hilda Miller and Ensemble
Plain We Live	Papa Yoder and Ensemble
The Shunning	The Company

ACT TWO

How Do You Raise A Barn?	Papa Yoder, Ezra Reber, Emma Miller, Samuel Zook and Ensemble
Follow Your Heart	Peter Reber, Katie Yoder and Hilda Miller
City Mouse, Country Mouse	Emma Miller with Sarah, Esther, Mary, Rachel, Rebecca

PLAIN AND FANCY

I'll Show Him!   Hilda Miller
Carnival Ballet   Hilda Miller, Ezra Reber and Company
  On The Midway
    Mambo Joe   Samuel Zook
    Scranton Sal   Dancer
    Swami   Another Amish Man
    Sailor   Jacob Yoder
    Barkers   Samuel Lapp, Abner Zook, Dancer
  Dance Hall   The Company
Take Your Time and Take Your Pick   Hilda Miller, Dan
                                King, Ruth Winters

Finale: Plenty of Pennsylvania   The Company

To Her, with love

JOE
WILL
ARNOLD

ACT ONE

ACT ONE

SCENE I

Country road in an Amish community in Lancaster County, Pennsylvania. PAPA YODER *is a stern, dignified Amishman in his middle fifties.* KATIE, *his daughter, is a gentle, attractive girl, about twenty years old.* PAPA YODER *and* KATIE *are driving in a typical Amish buggy.*

KATIE

We're almost home, Papa.

PAPA YODER

Yah! You must be tired from riding, Katie.

KATIE

Not so.

PAPA YODER
(Looking off)
Is that Ezra in the cabbage field?

KATIE

I don't think so. Maybe Ezra would not be working today.

PAPA YODER

Why not?

3

KATIE

Possible he is getting ready for the wedding.

PAPA YODER

Getting ready? The wedding is not for two days yet. What is there to get ready today?

KATIE

Well, maybe getting his clothes fixed up, maybe taking a bath . . .

PAPA YODER

Since when does a girl think of a man taking a bath "nokkid"?

KATIE

Papa, I did not mean it like that, I meant . . .

PAPA YODER

I'm sorry already I took you to Lancaster.

KATIE

Papa, just once before a girl gets married, she has a right to go by a big city.

PAPA YODER

A right, she says! A right! Your mama didn't go to Lancaster 'til she was forty-eight years old.

KATIE

I know, Papa.

4

PAPA YODER

A year later she was dead.

KATIE

Please, Papa.

PAPA YODER

Who knows what germs she caught there!

KATIE

Papa, don't talk so sad. I enjoyed to be in Lancaster. So many people. And everybody talking and laughing.

PAPA YODER

They are foolish people. In all Lancaster they do not even grow a turnip.

KATIE

And all those automobiles shlitzing up and down the streets. Were you ever in an automobile, Papa?

PAPA YODER
(Startled)

Me?

KATIE

I thought maybe sometimes . . .

PAPA YODER

Your cousin Abel was one time in an automobile . . .

KATIE

(*She has heard this before*)

I know, Papa . . .

PAPA YODER

Two and a half years later, dead in his grave!

KATIE

Papa, please . . .

PAPA YODER

It was the gasoline stink! Ate up his lungs . . .

KATIE

Papa, today just, let's talk about happy things only.

PAPA YODER

Yah! Ezra is a good man for you, Katie. . . . A good farmer. . . . And it's a fine piece of land I'm buying for him.

KATIE

It will be nice, Papa, ain't? . . . You on one farm, us on the farm right next. Later someday it will be one big farm.

PAPA YODER

Someday ain't yet. I ain't dead already!

KATIE

I didn't mean it that way, Papa, I meant . . .
(*Music begins for "It Wonders Me"*)

PAPA YODER

I know, Katie, I know. . . . I wish you could see how
happy you look. . . .

KATIE

I am happy. It was such a day. . . .

It wonders me,
It wonders me,
So beautiful a day can be,
So green the field,
So blue the sky,
So red and gold the maple tree.
Somewhere a breeze begins to sing
Somewhere a bird is answering,
So wonderful sweet the melody,
It wonders me.
    (*Music continues,* ENSEMBLE *enter and are seen in
    silhouette, in background*)
So green the field,
So blue the sky,
So gold the tree,
It wonders me.

PAPA YODER

Before a wedding, it is right for a girl to be happy. . . .

KATIE

Yah, Papa.

PAPA YODER

It will be nice Katie, ain't?

7

KATIE

I hope. I want it to be nice. Like today is nice.

(KATIE *and* ENSEMBLE *sing*)

(CHORUS *sings*)

It wonders me,
It wonders me,
So beautiful a day can be

(KATIE *sings*)

So green the field,
So blue the sky,
So red and gold the maple tree

(CHORUS *sings*)

Somewhere a breeze begins to sing

(KATIE *and* CHORUS *sing*)

Somewhere a bird is answering,
So wonderful sweet the melody,
It wonders me.

So green the field,
So blue the sky,
So gold the tree,
It wonders me.

Scene II

Section of road on the outskirts of a small town in Penn-sylvania. RUTH WINTERS *sitting in convertible,* DAN KING *leaning against fender, reading road map.* RUTH *is a bright, sharp, sophisticated New Yorker.* DAN *is good-looking, intelligent, very earnest, given to eager enthusiasm. They are both in their early thirties. At the moment* RUTH *is weary and slightly annoyed, after a tiresome car trip.*

RUTH

Dan, why don't you ask somebody?

DAN

This is route 27, isn't it?

RUTH

That sign said 27A.

DAN

That's the same as 27.

RUTH

Dan, I feel that A is important. Please ask somebody!

DAN

Don't worry, we'll find it!

9

RUTH

We'll never be heard from again!

DAN

I'm sure it's on this road somewhere. Come on, let's get back in the car.

RUTH

Relax. We've been in the car for days! Why didn't you sell your farm through a real estate agent?

DAN

My grandfather lived on that farm. I want to take a look at it before I sell it. Besides, I figured there might be a story on these Amish. They're fascinating people.

RUTH

You just wrote a story for *Cosmopolitan* on the Pennsylvania Dutch.

DAN

Honey, that was not the Pennsylvania Dutch. It was the Philadelphia Athletics. . . .

RUTH

Dan, I swear we've been on this road before! What have you got against asking somebody?

DAN

Who? In the last hour we've passed three pigs and a mail truck!

RUTH

Who gets mail around here? Do the pigs write to each other?

DAN

Don't worry, we'll find it. I bet we're practically on their doorstep.

RUTH

Well, at least we can have a drink. Dan, I've got a bottle of Scotch in my hatbox.

DAN

You'd better keep that bottle out of sight. The Amish are against drinking.

RUTH

Oh fine. Two days of buttermilk on the rocks! Why didn't you sell your property to that paper box outfit?

DAN

I couldn't do that to these people.

RUTH

They're against paper boxes, too?

DAN

A factory, Ruth . . . it would bring in thousands of strangers. The Amish want to be left alone.

RUTH

Good idea! Let's leave them alone and go back to New York.

DAN

You'll really enjoy meeting these people, Ruth. Just think of it. . . . They have had practically no contact with the outside world since they settled here in Lancaster County, and their customs haven't changed in all these two hundred years. It's inspiring in a way. The whole world changes around them but they stand solid with their simple honest values!

RUTH

(*Pausing*)
We can't even have one little drink?

DAN

No, they're really fascinating. Did I tell you about the buttons?

RUTH

Buttons? What buttons?

DAN

The Amish! They don't use buttons.

RUTH

How do they keep things closed? (*Looking off stage*) Dan, look, a people, a person . . . (ISAAC, *a short, bearded, brisk Amish man, enters*) Come on, I want to see if it's true about the buttons.

12

DAN

Ruth, please. (*To* ISAAC) Er . . . mister . . . sir . . . maybe you can help us. . . .

ISAAC

Yah?

DAN

We're looking for a family by the name of Yoder.

ISAAC

Yoder?

DAN

Yes. Do you know of a family by that name around here?

ISAAC

Yoder? There's maybe fourteen Yoder families.

DAN

I mean on this road.

ISAAC

I mean on this road.

DAN

We're looking for a Jacob Yoder. Is there a Jacob Yoder?

ISAAC

Sure.

DAN

Where can I find him?

ISAAC

Which one?

DAN

Is there more than one Jacob Yoder?

ISAAC

Four of them anyhow.

RUTH

(*To* DAN)

Let's get out of here.

DAN

Ruth, wait a minute. (*To* ISAAC) I have a letter here from Jacob Yoder.

ISAAC

Yah. (*Studies letter*) This is not from Fat Jacob Yoder over by Daisy Creek.

DAN

No?

ISAAC

He can't write.

RUTH

Three Jacob Yoders to go.

14

ISAAC

Maybe could it be Hairy Jacob Yoder with the two fingers missing?

RUTH

Oh my God. I hope not! . . . How is it there are so many Yoders around here?

ISAAC

Funny ain't? But not so funny like Zook.

RUTH

What's a Zook?

ISAAC

Also families like Yoder, only more. We got twenty-four families Zook.

DAN

Look, this Jacob Yoder has a daughter.

ISAAC

I know.

DAN

How do you know?

ISAAC

They all got daughters.

DAN

Oh?

ISAAC

Even the one who can't write.

DAN

Well, I understand this daughter is getting married soon.

ISAAC

Oh . . . Katie Yoder! That Jacob Yoder you're looking for?

DAN

I guess so.

ISAAC

He's my brother-in-law. Him you'll find down the road a piece. A house with an elm tree in front.

DAN

Thank you.
(ISAAC *starts to exit.*)

RUTH

By the way, what's that thing painted on that barn over there, a hex sign?

ISAAC

A hex?

RUTH

Well, I heard that around here, among the Pennsylvania Dutch . . .

16

ISAAC

That ain't a hex.
   (*He exits.*)

DAN

Ruth!

RUTH

What's the matter? What did I do now?

DAN

Did you have to mention hex? They don't like to discuss it
with outsiders.

RUTH

I'm sorry, but how would I know? I'm a Baptist! We have
no secrets from anyone. . . .

DAN

Come on . . . let's get back to the car. . . .
   (*Blackout and exit.*)

Scene III

The yard outside the Yoder home. The Yoder House is at the Right. Some girls are peeling potatoes in front of it. More girls are embroidering a tablecloth upstage center. Flowers are being potted. Apple butter is being churned. There is a wagon, and on it men are displaying vegetables. In front of them girls are peeling apples for the churn. Lights come up behind curtain for a tableau. Curtain flies open on music cue.

RACHEL

Emma, I have here some more apples.

EMMA

Good! (*As she adjusts wedding dress to* KATIE) It fits wonderful good, Katie. Ezra, what do you think of your beautiful bride?

EZRA

(*A crude, loud, muscular young man holds up basket*)
Look at the tomatoes—big like pumpkins!

EMMA

Ezra, look at Katie once! Forget the tomatoes!

EZRA

Such tomatoes I can't forget! . . . Look, Samuel. . . .
(KATIE *exits into house.*)

18

MAN

Emma, is there enough apple butter?

EMMA

I think we have enough of everything. What a beautiful time of year for a wedding!

(EMMA *and* ENSEMBLE *and* YOUNG MILLER GIRL *sing*)

(EMMA *sings*)
Winter is a good time,
Quieter than some.
You sit around the kitchen
And wait for spring to come.

(CHILDREN *sing*)
Chew your thumb and wait for springtime.

Spring is a good time,
Lilacs at the door,
Roses climbing up a garden wall.
Summer is a good time,
Time for things to grow,

(ENSEMBLE *sings*)
Time for getting ready
For the very best time of all—

(EMMA *sings*)
The fall.
Nights are crisp and the air like wine
And the leaves begin to burn,

And the dumbest Dutchman's doing fine
'Cause wherever you look
Wherever you turn is—

(EMMA *sings*)

Plenty of Pennsylvania.
You've never seen the likes of
Plenty of Pennsylvania
Where anything grows.

Plenty of Pennsylvania.
No pastures green the likes of
Plenty of Pennsylvania
Where anything grows.

All you need is some seed
And a plow or two,
And a bull who's keeping company
With a cow or two.

Soon you've got
Plenty of Pennsylvania,
Sweet land of meadows golden
And fat red barns for holdin'
What goes to town on market day.
Plenty of . . .
Plenty of Pennsylvan-i-ay.

(ENSEMBLE *sings*)

Anything grows in Pennsylvania.
Look around and you can see

Anything grows in Pennsylvania.
Anything and everything from A to Z.

Anything and everything from A to Z.

(CHILD *sings*)
Asparagus, broccoli, cauliflower,
Dandelion greens and escarole,
Fennel and grapes and honeydew melon
And iceberg lettuce for the salad bowl

(ENSEMBLE *sings*)
And iceberg lettuce for the salad bowl

(CHILD *sings*)
Juniper, kale and lovely lentils,
Mushrooms, nutmeg, okra, peas,
Quinces, rutabaga, squash, tomatoes,

(EMMA *sings*)
Un-i-ons sweet like strawberries
Vinegar . . . also watermelon
. . . Ex-plant planted all in rows

Yams and . . . zpinach?

No!

Zauerkraut?

No!

Zucchini!

(ENSEMBLE *sings*)

In Pennsylvania anything grows.

(*Repeat chorus*)

    (*Crowd talking.* DAN *and* RUTH *enter.*)

DAN

    (*Approaching an* AMISH WOMAN)

I beg your pardon . . . does a Mr. Yoder live here? (*The* AMISH WOMAN *doesn't answer, but looks shyly away.* DAN *goes to an* AMISH MAN) We're looking for a Mr. Jacob Yoder.

    (*The* MAN *stares at him and retreats.*)

RUTH

Well! It's been a lovely visit! Come on, Dan.

DAN

Wait a minute. Ruth . . .

    (HILDA *steps forward. About twenty-two, pert and attractive, she has a more self-confident manner than the others.*)

HILDA

You want Jacob Yoder?

DAN

That's right.

HILDA

He lives by here.

DAN

Oh. Are you Mrs. Yoder?

22

HILDA

(*Amused*)

No, I'm not yet anybody's missus. I am his niece, Hilda Miller. (*Two small children are half-hidden behind her skirts*) This is my sister and my brother.

(*The* CHILDREN *hastily retreat.*)

DAN

(*Looking around*)

Well, I'm sorry if we've interrupted a party or something. . . .

HILDA

(*Looking at him with real interest*)

Yah . . .

DAN

Perhaps we'd better come back some other . . .

HILDA

(*Quickly*)

No . . . stay once.

RUTH

If you're sure we're not in the way . . .

HILDA

No, no. (*Notices* RUTH's *attire*) Pardon me, please . . . are you a Spanish lady?

RUTH

Spanish . . . ?

23

HILDA

In a magazine once, I saw a Spanish lady wearing such a thing.

RUTH

Spanish? Honey, I bought this at Ohrbach's.

HILDA

(*Bewildered*)
Oh . . . (*Turns to* DAN, *fascinated*) You ain't a farmer, yet?

DAN

(*Amused*)
No, I'm not!

HILDA

(*Studies him for a moment, then in admiration, to herself*)
Golly, what a kind!

RUTH

(*Dryly*)
Yes . . .

DAN

Miss Miller, could you tell Mr. Yoder *I'm* here? I'm Dan King. We just drove down from New York.
(*There is a surprised rustle from the group.*)

HILDA

(*Turning, on porch*)
From New York, all the way to Bird-in-Hand?

24

PLAIN AND FANCY

RUTH

With a torn road map yet! (*Catches herself. To* DAN) *Yet?*
Iey, it's catching!

HILDA

(*To* DAN)
You're the fellow from the river farm, then.

DAN

..at's right.

HILDA

I didn't know such a fellow like you owned it.

DAN

Why? What sort of fellow did you expect?

HILDA

(*Slightly flustered*)
I thought an old . . . I mean . . . not so fancy . . .
Uncle Jacob is by the barn. Come in the house, once.

DAN

Thank you.
(*He exits into the house.* RUTH *starts to go into the
house, looks back and notices all the* Amish *staring at
her. She smiles at them reassuringly.*)

RUTH

No buttons! (*Slides side zipper of her skirt down and up*)
See? Zipper!
(*A murmur of amazement wells up among the Amish.*)

25

AMISH MAN

Did you see their car?

AMISH MAN

Without a top, even!

AMISH GIRL

Did you see the shoes she was wearing?

EMMA

(Entering from house)
Who was that Mexican lady?
(PETER *enters.*)

AMISH GIRL

Come, bring in the corn. . . .

AMISH MAN

Bessie, you bring the tomatoes and I'll bring the . . .
(*The talking stops as they all notice* PETER.)

PETER

Hello, Rachel!

RACHEL

You look nice, Peter. You fixed yourself by your Aunt. A little fatter.

PETER

Two years with Aunt Anna's cooking, why not? . . . Busy here.

EMMA

Everybody's bringing for your brother's wedding.

PETER

Oh! . . . Where's Katie?

SAMUEL

Hello, Peter, you came back.

PETER

Hello, Samuel.

SAMUEL

What a nice surprise.

PETER

Yah. Is Katie around?

SAMUEL

I guess. You were by the tobacco sale in Lebanon?

PETER

Yah. Where's Katie?

EMMA

Peter, Katie is getting married.

PETER

I know.

27

EMMA

Don't make trouble.

PETER

(*Crosses to* EMMA)
I only want to talk with her.

EMMA

Once you already got in trouble fighting about Katie. Again you want they should make you go away from here? Don't make trouble.
(PETER *starts to leave as* KATIE *enters from house.*)

KATIE
(*On porch*)

Peter!

PETER

Hello, Katie.

KATIE

I heard you came back.

PETER

Yah. This morning.

SAMUEL

(*Encouraging group to leave* KATIE *and* PETER *alone*)
Time for supper once, ain't?
(*He exits.*)

PLAIN AND FANCY

RACHEL

(Exiting)

Yah. Go wash.

(Others exit.)

KATIE

You look nice. A little thinner.

PETER

It was hard work by my uncle.

KATIE

(Coming down from porch)

They're all right, the family there?

PETER

The same. You look nice, too, Katie. Like always.

KATIE

(Steps away)

Thank you.

PETER

Are you happy, Katie?

KATIE

(Uneasily)

Yah. Sure.

PETER

Are you happy that you are getting married to Ezra?

KATIE

(*Looking away*)
You know, Peter, today I was by Lancaster.

PETER

I heard only yesterday about you and Ezra. I was surprised.
I hardly believed it.

KATIE

I have to go back inside. . . .
(*Starts to go.*)

PETER

Where is the promise we made . . . when we were children yet?

KATIE

We were so young, Peter. And you were away a long time.

PETER

I do not believe you forgot about us.

KATIE

I came to an age for marrying. And Papa . . .

PETER

Your Papa always liked Ezra. A good farmer.

KATIE

Yah, he is a good farmer!

30

PETER

And your Papa would never pick me for his Katie. Peter is a troublemaker . . . a man who fights, even.

KATIE

Please, Peter . . .

PETER

I fought only to keep Amos Beiler's hands off you!

KATIE

I know.

PETER

But your father did not care why.

KATIE

It's no use to talk about it now. . . .

PETER

Your father never cared why about anything. He saw me when I was plowing once, throw a stone in the river. I told him I wanted to watch the ripples only. He thought I was a crazy man. He heard me whistle once, and he told me to my face, "A man who whistles has an empty head!" This is not a man for his Katie.

KATIE

Peter, will you come to my wedding?

PETER

No. (*Crosses away from* KATIE) It would not make it happier if I came. I do not even have a proper present for you.

KATIE

Please . . . please come.

PETER

Remember the first present I gave you?

KATIE

(*Crosses to* PETER)

Yes. . . .

PETER

When you started in school . . . your first writing-book.

KATIE

And you drew a bluebird on the cover.

PETER

(*Smiling*)

With both eyes on one side of his head.

KATIE

Still I have it.

PETER

It was a silly thing . . . at that age to fall in love.

32

PLAIN AND FANCY

KATIE

Yes . . . it was.

PETER

But still you have it.

(He sings)

Once we were foolish children,
Playing as children play.
Racing through a meadow April bright,
Dreaming on a hilltop half the night.
Now that we're growing older,
We have no time to play.
Now that we're growing wiser,
We are not wise enough to stay . . .

Young and foolish,
Why is it wrong to be
Young and foolish,
We haven't long to be.
Soon enough the carefree days,
The sunlit days go by.
Soon enough the bluebird has to fly.
We were foolish,
One day we fell in love,
Now we wonder
What we were dreaming of,
Smiling in the sunlight,
Laughing in the rain,
I wish that we were young and foolish again.

(KATIE *is almost moved to kiss* PETER. *Music continues.*)

KATIE

(Drawing away)

No, Peter . . . no . . .
(She exits.)

(PETER *sings again*)
Smiling in the sunlight,
Laughing in the rain,
I wish that we were young and foolish again.

Scene IV

The Yoder parlor. It is typical of a prosperous Amish house-hold: stiffly furnished, obviously seldom used, very clean and austere. DAN, RUTH *and* HILDA *are sitting on a long settee. For a few moments no words are spoken but there are several strained smiles.*

DAN

(After pause)

I hope Mr. Yoder won't be tied up much longer.

HILDA

Tied up?

DAN

Busy. In the barn, with whatever he's doing.

HILDA

Oh, no. The new calf was yarrixing and he is taking care.

RUTH

(With interest)

Yarrixing?

35

HILDA

(Searching for the right word)

. . . Vomiting.

(RUTH *looks slightly ill.* PAPA YODER *and* ISAAC *enter. Throughout ensuing scene* HILDA *sits with hands primly folded in her lap.)*

PAPA YODER

Excuse me you're waiting till now.

DAN

That's quite all right, Mr. Yoder. I'm Dan King.

PAPA YODER

Hello.

DAN

And this is Miss Winters.

RUTH

How do you do!

PAPA YODER

How do you do! My brother-in-law.

RUTH

Didn't we talk to you on the road?

ISAAC

Yah. Coming from the store I was. They were coming from Ephrata a ways, and . . .

PAPA YODER

(*Cutting him off*)

Yah. (*To* DAN) I was busy by the barn. The new calf, today all day was yarrixing.

DAN

Yes, we heard the news. Mr. Yoder, you wrote me about buying my farm. . . .

PAPA YODER

Yah.

DAN

Well, as I was telling Miss Winters, I wanted to take a look at the place before I sold it.

PAPA YODER

(*Deliberately*)

Miss Winters? You're not married.

RUTH

No, we're not.

PAPA YODER

And you drove all the way here from New York together?

DAN

(*Bewildered*)

That's right.

PAPA YODER

(*This has condemned them*)

Yah! You're going back to New York today?

DAN

We hadn't planned to . . . it's a bit of a trip. Is there a hotel near here?

PAPA YODER

You came to sell the farm, ain't?

DAN

Yes. . . .

PAPA YODER

By us, people who visit don't go by a hotel. Stay here.

DAN

Oh, no . . . we don't want to impose . . .

PAPA YODER

No, there is for you a nice big bedroom in the back. (*To* RUTH) You sleep in the little room under the stairs.

RUTH

Little room under the stairs? Dan, why don't we go to a hotel? I'd love a hot tub, and . . .

PAPA YODER

A hot tub you can have here.

DAN

Just overnight, Ruth. Is my farm far from here, Mr. Yoder?

PAPA YODER

It is right past by my fence over by the river. With the big white barn.

(*The two little* MILLER CHILDREN *enter.*)

OLDER BOY

Uncle . . .

PAPA YODER

What?

OLDER BOY

The calf is again yarrixing.

PAPA YODER

(*Impatiently*)

Ach . . . I'll be a few minutes only.

(PAPA *and* CHILDREN *exit.*)

ISAAC

Mr. King, you got a good piece of land. He's buying it for his new son-in-law soon.

DAN

So I understand.

ISAAC

(*Sighs*)

By some people the daughter gets married, and by some people not.

(*Looks at* HILDA.)

HILDA

Papa . . .

ISAAC

(*Indicating* HILDA)

By her is a foolishness. Men come around by her plenty, but stay they don't.

(HILDA *grimaces slightly, indicating that this is an old story to her.*)

DAN

(*Slightly embarrassed*)

Well, I wouldn't worry about it, Mr. Miller.

ISAAC

She needs marrying. Twenty-two years yet. Children she should have now. But if there is no man, from where is the children?

RUTH

. . . A good question.

ISAAC

(*To* HILDA)

See? Even her, she says it.

DAN

Oh, I'm sure she'll get married, Mr. Miller. An attractive girl like Hilda.

(HILDA *smiles, pleased.*)

ISAAC

(*Still wound up*)

Moses Beiler wanted marrying.

DAN

He did?

ISAAC

Hot for her he was. But with her big mouth, she told him straight he is dumb like a cow.

HILDA

Moses Beiler *is* dumb like a cow.

ISAAC

(*Enraged*)

So? So you had to *tell* him?

HILDA

(*Placidly*)

Everybody knows. He should know, too, ain't?

DAN

Look, Mr. Miller . . .

ISAAC

(*To* DAN *and* RUTH)

And Jonas Fisher! A big wonderful built man! With ten acres of tobacco yet! He took her for rides in his buggy. All of a sudden is gefinished! (*Rhetorically*) Why?

HILDA

(*Looking straight ahead*)

Jonas Fisher sweats too much.

ISAAC

(*Furious*)

Every man sweats!

HILDA

Not like Jonas Fisher.

ISAAC

(*At wit's end*)

And this she *told* him!

HILDA

(*Demurely*)

Papa, you want me to be honest, ain't?

ISAAC

(*Exasperated*)

It is also honest not to be a blabbermaul! (*To* DAN) Excuse me that I holler, but with Hilda it boils me up. We don't see no man for her!

DAN

(*Uncomfortably*)

Yes! Well . . . er . . . if we're staying, I'll go out to the car and get our bags. Excuse me.

(KATIE *and* PAPA *enter in the middle of his speech.*)

42

ISAAC

This is Katie. For her is the wedding.

RUTH

Well! Congratulations, Katie!

KATIE

Thank you.

DAN

Mine, too, Miss Yoder.

PAPA YODER

From New York they are. From him I'm buying for you and
Ezra the river farm.

KATIE

Yes, Papa.

DAN

I'll bring the bags in.

RUTH

Be careful with my hatbox! Don't drop it!
    (DAN *exits.*)

ISAAC

    (*He looks at* RUTH *for a moment*)
Excuse me for asking . . .

RUTH

Yes?

ISAAC

Are you maybe a Gypsy lady?

RUTH

No, Mr. Miller. I bought this at a place in New York. . . .
(PETER *enters.*)

PETER

Mr. Yoder.

PAPA YODER

What are you doing here? In my house?

PETER

Mr. Yoder, I want to talk with you.

PAPA YODER
(*Coldly*)

About what?

PETER
(*Looks at* KATIE)
Alone I would like to talk with you.

KATIE

Peter . . .
(*She starts crossing to him.*)

PAPA YODER
(*Holds her back*)
We have nothing to talk. Go out of this house!

44

PETER

Mr. Yoder, you must listen to me once. . . .

PAPA YODER

Wherever you go comes trouble. (*Sharply*) I want you out of my house!
(PETER *looks at* PAPA YODER *for a moment, and exits left.* KATIE *starts to exit.*)

PAPA YODER

Katie! You and Hilda go and red up the rooms for the company. (KATIE *hesitates, then exits right.* HILDA *exits with her, her arm around* KATIE) Isaac, come help me with the calf.
(*He exits.*)

ISAAC

(*To* RUTH)
Yah! Miss, you want to come see the sick calf?

RUTH

No, thank you, but give him my best. . . .
(ISAAC *starts to exit as six stolid, heavy-set, bearded* AMISHMEN *enter. They troop in, and their eyes are immediately concentrated on* RUTH.)

ISAAC

Ah, look who came around once! Hello!

JACOB YODER

We left the pots and dishes in the kitchen. Anything more we can help?

45

ISAAC

The fixings are all, but stay a little.
(*They all look at* JACOB *for a decision.*)

JACOB

All right. A little.

ISAAC

We have with us this lady from New York . . . er . . .
Miss . . .

RUTH

Ruth Winters.

ISAAC

Make the acquaintance of some friends here. Wonderful
live fellows! (*She looks at them and they stare at her.* ISAAC
goes down the line) Abner Zook . . . Samuel Lapp . . . Ike
Pilersheim . . . Moses Zook . . . Abner Zook . . . and
Jacob Yoder. Nice fellows!
(*He exits.*)

RUTH

(*Recognition*)
Jacob . . . Oh! How do you do?
(RUTH *and* MEN *are left standing: after a moment, she
sits and they remain standing.*)

RUTH

(*Waves vaguely*)
Sit down, gentlemen.
(*They look to* JACOB.)

46

JACOB

We only stay a little.

RUTH

Yes . . . well . . . (*Sitting alone is awkward, and she rises*)
I'm only staying a little myself. (*There is a huge gap in the
conversation, and* RUTH *makes an effort*) It's lovely country
around here. . . . (*They don't answer. She struggles on*)
. . . it was lovely country all the way from New York . . .
(*Same kind of meager reaction*) . . . in fact, it's all lovely,
the whole country . . . from New York right to California
. . . (*Desperate*) . . . I just love America! (DAN *enters, carrying bag and a hatbox.* RUTH *crosses to him*) Where have
you been for the past three hours?

DAN

(*Glances at the men*)
Why? What's the matter?

RUTH

You'll find out. (*Cheerily turns to men*) Gentlemen, I'd like
you to meet Dan King. (*They nod*) Dan, this is . . . er . . .
er . . . Emile Schultz, I think . . .

AMISH MAN

Abner Zook.

RUTH

Of course . . . there are two of those. And this is (*Hesitates*) . . . Franz Shubert?

47

AMISH MAN

Samuel Lapp.

RUTH

I'm sorry . . . And this is the other one, Abner Zook . . .

AMISH MAN

Ike Pilersheim.

RUTH

That's right. Sorry, Ike. *This* is the other Abner Zook.

AMISH MAN

Moses.

RUTH

Oh, yes! Abner Moses!

AMISH MAN

Moses Zook.

RUTH

I could have sworn there were two Abners. And this gentle-
man is . . . er . . . Hammacher Schlemmer?

AMISH MAN

Abner Zook.

RUTH

(*To* DAN)

And you thought I was making it up! (*Up to the last one*)
And Dan, *guess* who this is? . . . Jacob Yoder!

48

DAN

Oh? . . . Oh! How do you do . . . !

RUTH

Not Fat Jacob Yoder. Not Hairy Jacob Yoder. This is Jolly Jacob Yoder!

DAN

I'm delighted to meet you, gentlemen. Why don't we all sit down?

RUTH

Dan, I've been through all that. They only stay a little.

DAN

Oh! . . . (*To* AMISH MEN) It's lovely country around here . . .

RUTH

I'll save you a lot of time. (*To* MEN) He loves America, too!

DAN

What?

RUTH

Come on, let's get unpacked. . . . (*They start to exit*) Well, fellows . . . keep the joint jumping!

    (*As* RUTH *and* DAN *start to exit*, EZRA *enters, carrying large cabbage.*)

DAN

Oh! Hello . . . (EZRA *stares at them, a little surprised*) I suppose you're another wedding guest.

EZRA

I'm not a guest. I'm the one getting married.

DAN

Oh! Wonderful.

RUTH

Congratulations!

DAN

(As EZRA *continues staring*)
Yes . . . er . . . that's certainly a fine cabbage you have there.

EZRA

It's rotten!

DAN

Well . . . that's the way the world spins. . . . Come on, Ruth. . . .
(*They exit.* ALL *look after them.* EZRA *shakes his head as he studies cabbage.*)

JACOB

What are you so grumpy?

EZRA

My cabbages are all yellow by the edges.

JACOB

A man gets married Thursday should smile a little.

50

PLAIN AND FANCY

EZRA

Thursday I'll smile. Maybe.

SAMUEL LAPP

Ezra . . . you're glad to marry Katie, ain't?

EZRA

What's to be so glad?

ABNER ZOOK

You're not glad?

EZRA

What's not to be glad?

SAMUEL LAPP

So why are you marrying Katie?

(EZRA *sings*)
Comes a time in his life
When a man should take a wife.
If I have to take a wife,
So why not Katie?

Milking cows Katie knows,
Katie mends and Katie sews,
And a farm with Katie goes,
So why not Katie?

It could be if I wait
Comes along a perfect mate,

But for this a man could wait
Until he's eighty.

So in meeting when I stand
With my hand in Katie's hand
And a wedding dinner making in the pot,
When they ask, "Do you take Katie?"
I will answer like a shot:
"Do I take Katie . . . ?
Why not?"

    (AMISH ONE *sings*)
She's a nice girl, Katie always was.

    (EZRA *sings*)
When her father says "Shut up" to her, she always does.

    (AMISH TWO *sings*)
You could marry Bertha Broder, like a dream she cooks,

    (AMISH THREE *sings*)
Like an ox she's healthy,

    (EZRA *sings*)
Like an ox she looks.

    (AMISH FOUR *sings*)
Kate's a bissel skinny where she should be fat.

    (EZRA *sings*)
When the kids start coming, she won't be so flat.

52

PLAIN AND FANCY

(AMISH FIVE *sings*)

With the hand of Anna Gruber comes a lot of cash.

(EZRA *sings*)

With the face of Anna Gruber comes a big mustache.

(AMISH SIX *sings*)

Once you promised Ilsa Brett
When she grew up, you she'd get,

(EZRA *sings*)

But she ain't stopped growing yet,
So I'll take Katie.

(AMISH THREE *sings*)

Once I kissed Dora Brand,
I found schmutzing Dora grand.

(EZRA *sings*)

So did half of Bird-in-Hand,
So I'll kiss Katie.

(EZRA *sings*)

It could be if I wait
Comes along a perfect mate,
But for this a man could wait
Until he's eighty.

So tomorrow when I stand
With my hand in Katie's hand
And in meeting house they put me on the spot,

In a clear and honest voice
Since I ain't got no other choice
I'll answer: "Katie . . . !"

(AMISH MEN *sing*)
Sweet and lovely Katie . . . !

(EZRA *sings*)
Hard-working Katie!
Why not?

SCENE V

Behind the Yoder house.
It is early evening.
KATIE *enters carrying copybook, with a picture of a blue-*
bird on it. Two young couples pass her in romantic attitudes.

FIRST COUPLE
Hello, Katie.
> (KATIE, *preoccupied, acknowledges them with a nod.*
> *She goes to, and sits on, bench. After a moment* DAN
> *enters.*)

DAN
Good evening, Katie.

KATIE
Oh. Hello.
> (*She closes the book and holds it on her lap.*)

DAN
I thought I'd take a look at my river farm. It's not far, is it?

KATIE
(Rising)
No. If you want, I'll show you.

DAN
No hurry. That was a wonderful dinner, Katie.

55

KATIE

I'm glad you enjoyed.

DAN

That meat dish. I remember my grandmother used to make it. What do you call it again?

KATIE

Kassler Ripschen und Sauerkraut.

DAN

Your future husband is getting a great cook.

KATIE

Yah. That he knows.
(*Looks away.*)

DAN

Is anything the matter? Are you all right?

KATIE

I am all right. Sure.

DAN

You don't seem very happy . . . the day before your wedding.

KATIE

I am happy. Of course I am happy. Ezra is good Amish. Never does he make trouble. Why should I not be happy?

DAN

Of course. How long have you two been engaged?

KATIE

It's maybe three months since Papa and Ezra's papa decided.

DAN

I see. That's the way it was arranged.

KATIE

Yah.

DAN

And you'll be living on the farm I'm selling your father.

KATIE

I guess.

DAN

(*Awkwardly*)

Well . . . I hope you'll be very happy.

KATIE

Thank you!

DAN

(*Notices book*)

What's that on the cover?

KATIE

This? A bluebird. It's my old schoolbook.

DAN

(Takes book)

Curious-looking thing. May I see it? Two eyes on one side
of its head.

(Looks at her.)

KATIE

(Turning away)

Somebody made it for me once.

DAN

A boy?

KATIE

Yah.

DAN

(Glances at her; leafs through book)

You weren't too good in arithmetic, Katie.

KATIE

No.

DAN

(Still leafing through)

Say, this poem is charming. Did you write it?

KATIE

No, it's from around here. *(Hesitates)* Somebody wrote it
in for me.

DAN

Oh. The artist?

58

KATIE

(*Hesitates*)

Yah.

(*The music of "Young and Foolish" plays very quietly
during the following scene.*)

DAN

(*Reads*)

"I love you so and we can get a house
And you can fix it nice with paint . . .
And when the stars is out, we'll feel so fine,
But when the stars is all, you'll love me . . . ain't?"

(*Long pause.*)

KATIE

(*Rises*)

I'll show you the farm.

(*They exit. Music continues as the lights fade.*)

Scene VI

The Barn on River Farm. PETER, *on ladder, painting blue-bird in profile, two eyes on one side of head.* DAN *and* KATIE *enter. As they speak,* PETER *hears them, descends ladder.* DAN *is still carrying* KATIE's *book.*

KATIE

. . . and over that hill is the river.

DAN

Beautiful land. And all that is tobacco . . . !

KATIE

Corn!

DAN

I'd better brush up on my botany! But you do grow tobacco here.

KATIE

Yah. Also grows here a lot of . . .
(*Sees* PETER.)

PETER

Hello, Katie.

60

KATIE

Peter! You shouldn't have . . . This is Mr. King. Peter
Reber.

DAN

How do you do.

PETER

Hello.

DAN

That's an interesting bird you're painting there.

PETER

(*Looking at* KATIE)

Yah.

DAN

These barn decorations are very colorful and . . . (*Looks
at book cover, looks at painting on barn, realizes significance.
Hands book back to* KATIE) I'd better get back to the house.
. . . Ruth is waiting for me. Nice meeting you, Peter!
(DAN *exits.*)

KATIE

You should not have done it, Peter!

PETER

I'm going away, Katie. Tonight. I wanted you should remember me.

61

KATIE

You should not have done it.

PETER

If you want I will paint it over.

KATIE

No . . . don't. Peter, you don't have to go away.

PETER

I want to!

KATIE

Peter . . . ! Please don't go away.

PETER

Katie . . . Katie?

KATIE

(*Rushing to his arms*)
Don't go away from me again, Peter!

PETER

I will talk to your father! He must listen to me!

KATIE

Not you, Peter. I will talk to him. To me he will listen.

PETER

You think, Katie?

62

KATIE

He must! I will make him listen! He must believe that you
are good Amish. And you will be, ain't, Peter?

PETER

Yes, Katie.

KATIE

Not for Papa only. For me. Fighting is sinful. Promise me,
Peter . . . never again . . . promise!

PETER

Never again. I promise!
(*They embrace.*)

KATIE

Like it was a long time ago, ain't?

PETER

The best time it was. . . .

(KATIE *sings*)

Young and foolish,
It can't be wrong to be
Young and foolish,
We haven't long to be.
Soon enough the carefree days, the sunlit days go by.
Soon enough the bluebird has to fly.

63

(PETER *sings*)
Call me foolish,
But I would choose to be
Young and foolish,
The way we used to be.

(BOTH *sing*)
Smiling in the sunlight, laughing in the rain,
Together we'll be young and foolish again.

They exit. Young Amish girls and boys enter, carrying lanterns. By lantern light boys and girls dance.

Scene VII

Small bedroom in Yoder home. It has a slanting ceiling, as if under stairs. It is sparsely furnished: a bed, dresser, hooks on wall, a curtain strung on a pole, no mirror or pictures. Ruth's hatbox is on the bed, open. RUTH *is sprawled in hard-backed chair, smoking and with a drink in her hand.*

RUTH

(Bitterly)

To Hairy Jacob Yoder . . . ! (*She drinks, takes a more relaxed puff. Looks at cigarette, starts looking around for a place to drop the ashes. There is no ashtray; she considers flicking ashes into her palm . . . holds top of her dress out for a moment, rejects this idea . . . looks around room, gets increasingly irritated, starts to go to dresser, when she hits her head on ceiling*) This room was built for an Amish midget! (*Knock at door*) Who is it?

DAN

(Entering)

Hi . . . Just wanted to see if you were comfortable.

RUTH

Sure! . . . I don't know why I let you drag me down here. . . .

65

DAN

Now wait a minute . . . I didn't drag you. I asked you if you wanted to come, and you said yes.

RUTH

Well, I thought you'd have been disappointed if I'd refused.

DAN

Oh, I would have been. Very.

RUTH
(*Warmly*)

Would you, Dan?

DAN
(*Warmly*)

Of course. . . . (*A pause. Looks at chest*) I bet this chest is over two hundred years old.

RUTH
(*Dryly*)

That's just what I was thinking!

DAN

Well, I'm going to get unpacked. Anything you want?

RUTH

Nothing I can think of!

66

PLAIN AND FANCY

DAN

See you later. . . .
> (*He exits. She looks after him, and starts singing.*)

In natural history every he
When wanting a particular she
Can always find a way to tell her so.
The cricket chirps, the penguin struts,
The monkey tosses coconuts,
The bullfrog makes a noise like Vaughn Monroe.
What's true of bird and beast and bee
Applies to people equally
Except for my particular Romeo.

He may adore me—how would I know?
If I'm the light of his life,
It doesn't show.
I go through the motions but I'm well aware
It's a helluva way to run a love affair.

He doesn't tingle whenever we meet,
Our love has all the thrill
Of shredded wheat.
We never run barefoot through each other's hair;
It's a helluva way to run a love affair.

Some lucky lovers have a talent for romance;
Hackensack can seem like Paris, France.
I have a true love with a diff'rent kind of knack;
He turns Paris into Hackensack.

I'm not suggesting he isn't A-1
He has a character like . . . George Washington
But when will my Georgie cross the Delaware?
It's a helluva way to run a love affair.

I try to lure him with romantic atmosphere,
Candlelight and music in his ear.
I whisper lyrics that speak love in every line,
And he falls in love with Oscar Hammerstein.

For no good reason I'm hanging around,
There must be some other fish that can be found.
I'm stuck with the one I'm stuck on . . . *c'est la guerre*,
My trustworthy, loyal, helpful, friendly . . . square,
But it's a helluva way to run a love affair.
(*After song,* RUTH *goes to the dresser for her cigarette.
There is a knock on the door.*)

RUTH

Just a minute. Just a minute! (*She drinks down her un-
finished Scotch, recaps the bottle and puts it in her hatbox.
Another knock on the door*) In a second . . . who is it? (RUTH
*becomes aware of the cigarette in her hand, can't decide what
to do with it and holds it behind her back when there is another knock at the door*) Yes . . . who is it?
(HILDA *enters.*)

HILDA

Excuse me. You ready for your bath?

RUTH

I'd love it.

HILDA

It will be ready soon now.

RUTH

Fine. By the way, Hilda, this room doesn't seem to have a closet.

HILDA

No, we use the hooks. (*Sniffs*) Something is brenning!

RUTH

Brenning?

HILDA

From a fire it smells!

RUTH

(*Takes cigarette from behind back*)
Oh, that's this.

HILDA

(*Shocked*)
You were smoking it?

RUTH

Well . . . yes. I . . .

HILDA

(*Awed*)
Uncle Jacob would have a conniption.

RUTH

I'm sorry.

HILDA

(*Conspiratorial*)
But what he don't know won't conniption him.

RUTH

(*Looks at her with new regard*)
Right!
(RUTH *takes final puff.*)

HILDA

(*Extending hand*)
I will throw it away.

RUTH

(*Gives her butt*)
Do Amish men smoke?

HILDA

(*Crosses to window, looks out carefully before throwing
butt out*)
Some do. Young ones. But no woman ever. She would be
shunned.

RUTH

What do you mean?

HILDA

Shunned. No one talks to you or looks at you or anything.
Shunned is a terrible thing. (*Picks* RUTH's *dress from bed*)
You want I should hang you up?

RUTH

Thank you, dear. (*The door opens and the two children enter carrying a wooden tub. They set it down*) Well sir, madam . . . what is this?

HILDA

For your bath. (*To the children*) Get the hot water.
(*They stand and stare at* RUTH, *as* RUTH *stares at the tub.*)

HILDA
(*Sharply*)

Move once!
(*They run out of the room.*)

RUTH

Hilda . . . no indoor plumbing?

HILDA

By us plain Amish, such a thing is not allowed.

RUTH
(*Incredulous*)

Nobody has plumbing?

HILDA

Well . . . a few fancy ones.

RUTH

I see. The button crowd! . . . Well! Bath time!
(*Pulls tub behind curtain. Starts undressing behind curtain. It is about shoulder high.*)

71

HILDA

I'll finish putting away for you. (*Picks up dress*) Golly, what soft goods.

> (*During ensuing dialogue,* HILDA *is emptying suitcase and putting clothes away.* RUTH *throws slip, etc. on screen wire.*)

HILDA

(*Picks up sheer panties from wire and stares at them*)
What is this?

RUTH

(*Looks over curtain*)
Panties. . . . You know, underwear.

HILDA

Oh . . . these go under the bloomers.

RUTH

Bloomers? I don't wear bloomers.

HILDA

(*Astounded*)
Just . . . these? . . .

RUTH

That's all.

HILDA

This would give Mama a conniption. . . . The shoes I'll put under the bed here.

RUTH

Fine.

HILDA

(*After a moment*)
You are keeping company with Mr. King steady-like?

RUTH

Dan? Hmmm . . . no. Not what you'd call steady-like.

HILDA

He is a very interesting-looking man.

RUTH

Yes, he is.

HILDA

He's wonderful nice.

RUTH

Mm. I hope this tub doesn't give me any splinters any-where.

HILDA

I looked at Mr. King's fingers already. They are very clean.

RUTH

Yes.

HILDA

Like a dentist! (*As she picks up brassière from wire*) Very polite he is also, and . . . (*Notices bra*) . . . what is this thing?

73

RUTH

(*Looks over curtain*)
What do you think it is?

HILDA

(*Examining it, holds it by ends, so that it looks like a basket*)
For carrying things?

RUTH

No, dear, it . . . well, in a way! Look, it's for . . . (*Indicates on herself with a little clumsy embarrassment*) You wear it. Around here.

HILDA

It's wonderful fancy! (*Taking Scotch bottle out of hatbox*) You want I should put this away for you?

RUTH

That? No, dear, I'll put that away myself.

HILDA

(*Holds up brightly colored dress*)
Look at this once!

RUTH

You like it? It's yours!

HILDA

Me? How could I wear this ever?
(*She puts dress on hook. The two children enter.*)

74

HILDA

So where is the water?

BOY

Papa wants the tub once.
(The BOY *starts to go behind curtain.)*

RUTH
(Yelps)

Wait a minute once!
(Hastily puts on robe as children retreat. She comes out from behind curtain. The children pick up the tub.)

HILDA

Where are you going to take the tub?

BOY

The sick calf . . . Papa wants to wash him down.

RUTH

(Coming out from behind curtain)
But what about my bath?

BOY

You can take a bath after the calf.
(The children start to exit with tub, staring at RUTH.*)*

RUTH

Forget it! Don't bring it back . . . ever!
(The children exit.)

75

HILDA

By the kitchen sink you can wash a little.

RUTH

That'll have to do.

HILDA

(*After a moment*)

It wonders me something.

RUTH

What is it now . . . the girdle?

HILDA

It wonders me that a person like you, with such a pretty face, is not yet married.

RUTH

Well, I was married.

HILDA

Oh. He died by you, the husband?

RUTH

No, but it's a lovely idea. We were divorced.

HILDA

(*Amazed*)

Divorced yet!

RUTH

Hilda, where is the—er . . . ladies room . . . the—er . . .

76

HILDA

(*Simply*)

The toilet?

RUTH

You do talk loud and clear, don't you? Where is it?

HILDA

Outside, in the back.

RUTH

I should have known. (DAN *enters as* RUTH *starts to exit*)
Hello, Clean Fingers!

DAN

Where are you going?

RUTH

Outside, in the back . . . Stay a little yet, already, anyhow, yet, once.

(RUTH *exits.*)

HILDA

Mr. King . . .

DAN

(*Turns back*)

Yes, Hilda?

HILDA

Er . . . you want I should help in your room?

77

DAN

No, thanks, everything's all right. (*Starts out, then turns back*) Oh, Hilda . . .

(HILDA, *flustered, starts to fix bed.*)

HILDA

Yah, Mr. King?

DAN

(*Hesitantly*)
Who is this fellow Peter?

HILDA

Peter? He is Ezra's brother.

DAN

I know, but I was wondering . . . about him and Katie.

HILDA

Oh. That. (*Busies herself with bed for moment*) They were ferliebt since they were kids yet.

DAN

Oh?

HILDA

But Katie's papa never liked him, and . . . (*She finds glass under pillow*) Look . . . under the pillow!

(*Sniffs at it, and reacts slightly.* DAN *takes glass and sniffs it.*)

DAN

Ruth's been taking her vitamins. I hope your father lets you marry a man you choose.

HILDA

I hope. It would be pleasant when you're marrying a man, you also like him.

DAN

(*Amused*)

That's true. And you have a pretty way of putting things.

HILDA

(*She is standing at window, turns to him*)

Pretty? Me?

DAN

I meant . . . yes, you are a pretty girl.

HILDA

I guess where you come from all the girls are pretty-like.

DAN

Where in the world did you get that idea?

HILDA

Sometimes they pass by here in their cars, and they're always so shiny.

DAN

The cars.

HILDA

The people too . . . you know? . . . Sometimes I think of how it is outside of here.

DAN

And how do you think it is?

HILDA

Well . . . everything is polished like silver . . . and people walk light . . . and there's a lot of laughing.

DAN

Don't you like it here, Hilda?

HILDA

Oh, yah. I like it fine. It is a happy life here.

DAN

But you think about other places. . . .

HILDA

Sometimes. I would like to see how it is maybe . . . once. Sometimes I see an airplane, and I think, what kind of man is up there, flying through the clouds? I guess a lean man, and tall, and without a beard. . . .

DAN

I see. . . .

80

HILDA

I think it is all like that. The girls are pretty and the men are tall and they move through the sky.

DAN

It isn't quite like that, Hilda. The men are not all tall, and the girls certainly aren't all as pretty as you are.

HILDA

You think?

DAN

I know. Not as pretty or as charming. The fellow who gets you will be very lucky.

HILDA

(Pauses, slightly flustered)
Also I cook good.

DAN

I know you do.

HILDA

(Hangs dress. Pauses)
Also children I like.

DAN

(Looks at her curiously)
Hilda, how old are you?

HILDA

I'm twenty-two.

DAN

Twenty-two. That's a wonderful age.

HILDA

You think? Papa worries I'm getting to be an old one.

DAN

Old? Why, you're young . . . and sweet and radiant.

HILDA

What does that mean?

DAN

Why . . . full of life; refreshing . . .

HILDA

Refreshing?

DAN

Well, that means . . .

HILDA

I think it means you like me, ain't?
(*By now her face is close to his.*)

DAN

(*Takes her face in his hands*)
Of course I do. You're . . . I guess the right word is . . .
enchanting.

HILDA

What does that mean?

DAN

It means . . .
> (*He kisses her lightly. Turns and exits.* HILDA *looks after him*)

> (*She sings*)

All at once the room is reeling,
Bells are pealing,
Butterflies are fluttering inside.
All at once I get to feeling
Just like a new-born bride . . .
> (*She comes down front. Curtain closes, boys and girls start entering*)

This is all very new to me,
This is all very fine,
This so sunny-like,
Sort of funny-like,
Milk-and-honey-like feeling of mine.
This is all very new to me,
And I'm knocking on wood.
What to do? What to say?
How to make it go on this way?
Wish that I understood
'Cause it feels oh so good!

> (GIRLS *sing*)

Do you seem to float in space?

(HILDA *sings*)
With the silliest look on my face
And a light in my eye.

(GIRLS *sing*)
Do you feel all out of breath?

(HILDA *sings*)
Upside-down, scared to death

(GIRLS *sing*)
Are you wondering why?

(HILDA *sings*)
It's as simple as pie.
(*Curtain opens on Yoder yard for second chorus and
production dance number. Wedding guests arrive
during number and ensuing scene*)

(HILDA *sings*)
This is all very new to me,
Has me all in a haze.

(GIRLS *sing*)
Now you know about
What they glow about.

(HILDA *sings*)
And I go about shouting its praise.
This is all very new to me
And I'm knocking on wood.
What to do? What to say?

84

How to make it go on this way?
Wish that I understood
'Cause it feels oh so good!
So wonderful good!

    (*Dance*)

What to do? What to say?
How to make it go on this way?
Wish that I understood
'Cause it feels oh so good!
So wonderful good!

Scene VIII

Yoder yard. Amish men and women cross to right, dressed in "best" clothes. . . . They continue crossing during scene. EZRA *crosses with chairs to house.*

FIRST AMISH MAN

(*To his wife*)

See? There's still more buggies coming. I told you we're not late!

FIRST AMISH WOMAN

(*To second woman*)

You heard? Amos Lapp and all are coming for the wedding Thursday all the way from Lebanon.

(PAPA *and* DAN *enter from left.*)

PAPA YODER

. . . So tell me your price. I am ready to pay cash.

DAN

Mr. Yoder, you don't have to pay the whole thing in cash. I don't mind taking a mortgage for part of it.

PAPA YODER

We don't like mortgages. If we ain't got cash we don't buy.

SAMUEL

Jacob, hello! This time next year you'll be a grandfather!

86

PAPA YODER

I hope. Go inside. Everybody's by the parlor.

DAN

You're having quite a few visitors tonight.

PAPA YODER

Before a wedding, people visit, to enjoy a little. (*Pause*)
Yah. On the river farm, they will have a happy life, Katie and
Ezra.

DAN

I hope so . . .

PAPA YODER

Twenty-five acres, and a good big house. I always wanted
to do the best for Katie.

DAN

Well . . . Mr. Yoder, I don't think Katie's marrying the
man she really wants.

PAPA YODER

What are you talking? Who does she want?

DAN

She's in love with Peter, Mr. Yoder.

PAPA YODER

That one! A troublemaker. He was sent away from here
for making trouble, for fighting. In love . . . she wants . . . !

87

AMISH MAN

Jacob, my cousin Aaron is here yet?

PAPA YODER

I guess. Or else not.
(*Amish man exits.*)

DAN

Just talk to her for a minute, Mr. Yoder. Why, when I saw
Peter painting that bird on the barn I was sure . . .

PAPA YODER

He painted a bird?

DAN

On the barn, on my property. Mr. Yoder, Katie and Peter
grew up together, they . . .

PAPA YODER

What kind of a bird?

DAN

Oh, I don't know. A thing with both eyes on one side of its
head. Look, I know all of this is none of my business, but . . .

PAPA YODER

That's a funny thing to paint where Ezra and Katie will
live . . .
(KATIE *enters.*)

KATIE

Papa. Can I talk to you once?

PAPA YODER

You saw Peter!

KATIE
(*Defiantly*)

Yes, I did!

PAPA YODER

I told you not to!

KATIE

But anyway I saw him. That is why I want to talk with you.

PAPA YODER

There is nothing to talk! Go into the house with the company.
(*Several* AMISH *cross.*)

AMISH WOMAN

Katie, wait till you'll see my wedding present! Come inside.

KATIE
(*Starting to exit*)

I will talk with you, Papa. If not now, later!
(*She exits.*)

PAPA YODER

That one had to come back!

DAN

Mr. Yoder, how can you force a girl to marry a man you've picked out for her?
(*Others start entering.*)

PLAIN AND FANCY

PAPA YODER

We do not force! A father knows only that he is smarter than a child yet.

DAN

But there's such a thing as being too strict.

PAPA YODER

Strict is our way of living, mister. Strict is how we live, and plain, and simple and content!

DAN

But look, Mr. Yoder, times have changed. You just can't . . .

(PAPA *and* AMISH MEN *sing*)
Let me say it once, mister,
We know how we want it here.
We know who we are, mister,
Don't interfere.
We don't need a city man, with city soft words,
To tell us what to do.
Go upon your way, mister,
We got our own way, too.

Plain We Live,
For plain we see.
It's good for people to live plain.
Hard we work so life is good.
When life is hard we don't complain.
Strangers look on us and call us strange
But cheat we don't and steal we don't
And wars we don't arrange.
Plain We Live

For plain is good
And plain is how we mean to stay.
To God we pray to keep us plain.

(PAPA YODER *recites*)

Look around you, mister! Look in your world, and look here! Poor people you have plenty, and worried people and afraid. Here we are not afraid. We do not have all your books, and your learning, but we know what is right. We do not destroy, we build only.

(PAPA *and* MEN *sing*)

Strangers look on us and call us strange
But cheat we don't and steal we don't
And wars we don't arrange.
Plain We Live
For plain is good
And plain is how we mean to stay.
To God we pray to keep us plain.

(*They exit at end of song leaving* DAN *alone.* PETER *enters. Throughout the ensuing dialogue, there is an occasional flash of summer lightning.*)

PETER

Mr. King . . .

DAN

What is it, Peter?

PETER

Mr. King, I want to buy your river farm.

DAN

You want to buy it?

91

PETER

Tell me how much, Mr. King! Almost three hundred dollars I have saved up. The rest I could pay off from the crops.

DAN

Peter, I told Mr. Yoder I'd sell it to him. That's why I came down here.

PETER

I hoped always someday to live on that farm . . . with Katie!

DAN

Peter, having the farm won't help you. Mr. Yoder wouldn't call off the marriage even if I didn't sell it to him.

PETER

I do not know. But I must try. Tell me only how much!
(*Thunder and lightning.* EZRA *enters.*)

EZRA

(*Good-naturedly*)
Peter! Give me a help once, will you? In the buggy there, I brought extra chairs for the company.

PETER

I am busy, Ezra. I am talking.

EZRA

(*To* DAN)
Did you finish with Mr. Yoder about the farm, yet?

DAN

Not yet.

EZRA

I'll have a job for you on the farm, if you want, Peter.

PETER

(*Irritated*)

I don't want.

EZRA

(*Crosses to* PETER *below wagon*)
You still ferhoodled about Katie? (PETER *does not answer.*)

(*To* DAN)

He is still feerhoodled about Katie. (*There is another flash of lightning and a loud clap of thunder*) It's going to come down soon rain. Don't stand like a lummox. Help out a little with the chairs. (PETER *turns away*) It's for the wedding, Peter. Katie's wedding. You always wanted to be by Katie's wedding, ain't? . . . So you'll be, but in the back! I'll be in the front. Don't be so ferhoodled about Katie. She's a girl like all girls. There are plenty of girls left for you. (*Laughs* . . . PETER *turns away*) Come on, pick up a chair, maybe I'll let you kiss the bride. . . . You'll enjoy to kiss Katie, ain't? . . . I'll let you kiss her, but no pinching!

(PETER, *raging, attacks him.* EZRA *falls to the ground and* PETER *pummels him.*)

DAN

(*Tries to pull* PETER *away*)

Peter, stop it! Let him go, this won't get you anywhere.

(EMMA, HILDA, PAPA, AMISH MEN *and* WOMEN *run out of house.*)

93

AMISH MAN

It's Peter. He's fighting again!

EMMA

Stop him, somebody!

SAMUEL

(*Pulling* PETER *away*)

Peter, stop! You can't fight your own brother!

KATIE

Peter, you promised . . . you promised.

EZRA

He's crazy, that one!

PAPA YODER

He is a man of violence!

AMISH MAN

(*Looking off*)

What is that over there?

EZRA

Where?

AMISH MAN

Look! Smoke.

SECOND AMISH MAN

Something is brenning!

SAMUEL

Looks like a haystack . . .

PAPA YODER

No! It's too big a fire for that.

EZRA

The barn. On your farm!

AMISH MAN

Jacob! We need buckets!

DAN

What can I do to help?

PAPA YODER

Quick, get buckets in my barn.

AMISH MAN

Also, we'll need axes.

SAMUEL

Get the animals out first.

PAPA YODER

Run over to the Rebers' and get help.

EMMA

Hilda! Find the children.

AMISH MAN

Where shall we bring everything?

PAPA YODER

Get the buckets. Save what you can! Bring everything into my barn!

(People rush off, including PAPA. *Landscape curtain closes. Men carrying sacks, buckets, etc.)*

MAN

Bring it in the Yoder barn!

MAN

Get more buckets!

*(*THIRD MAN *crosses over from right with buckets.* FOURTH *and* FIFTH MEN *cross over from left wearily carrying sacks, mopping brows.)*

FOURTH MAN

The smoke . . . you can't get in there no more!

THIRD MAN

(Rushing off)

We'll try to save something at least!

(Silhouette shows fire. People rush through. DAN *enters right with buckets.)*

DAN

Did they get the animals out?

96

FIFTH MAN

I think!
(*He exits.*)

HILDA

(*Entering left with two children*)
It's no use . . . it's no use . . . (*She stops* DAN) Don't go!
Nobody can go near it no more. . . . It's brenning terrible
fast.

DAN

(*Looking off*)
It went up like a matchbox!

HILDA

Yah . . . it started so sudden. How could it happen?

DAN

It must have been struck by lightning!

HILDA

I guess! (*To man with sack*) Bring it in the Yoder barn.
Everything we're bringing there.

DAN

Better get the kids into the house! I'll see if they need help
in the Yoder barn. . . .
(*Scene opens on Yoder barn. Some of the ensemble is
on stage. Others enter during scene.*)

PAPA YODER

(*Running into barn*)
Is everybody all right? Did anybody get hurt?

SAMUEL

No! I never saw anything go up so fast.

EZRA

(*Comes on from left*)
Mr. Yoder! The barn is all!

PAPA YODER

I know. I know also what made it!
    (*Glaring at* PETER. KATIE *in from right* . . . DAN *enters.*)

DAN

Probably struck by lightning!

PAPA YODER

It was a hex!

ALL

A hex . . .

PAPA YODER

His hex!

DAN

But, Mr. Yoder. That's ridiculous!

PAPA YODER

He is our trouble. We will manage it. We! Not you.

RACHEL

I seen the hex! It was a bluebird thing.

PETER

That was not a hex!

KATIE

That was not a hex, Papa.

PAPA YODER

(*To* PETER)

It was. You done it. You wanted her! Even your own brother you struck.

DAN

Now wait, Mr. Yoder!

PAPA YODER

(*To* PETER)

This is not the first time you have made trouble here. You are not a plain man. You have violence in you. For this, you will be punished . . . for this you will be shunned!

(DAN *looks at* HILDA *questioningly.*)

HILDA

Shunned. Is a terrible thing!

(*The ensemble on stage are frozen for a moment, staring at* PETER. DAN *starts to approach him, as if to help,*)

99

and HILDA *leads him off. The "Plain We Live" theme
starts quietly, and* AMISH MEN *and* WOMEN *slowly start
exiting, turning away from* PETER, *as they pass him.
The ensemble starts singing "Plain We Live," slowly
exiting as they shun* PETER. PETER *goes to* EZRA, *ap-
pealing to him, but* EZRA *turns from him and exits.*
SAMUEL *does the same.* PETER *looks toward* KATIE, *who
rushes toward him, wanting to embrace him. But as
she reaches him, she turns toward her father, remem-
bers her duty as an Amish girl, and exits, following*
PAPA YODER *off stage.* PETER *is left in center, and
male and female chorus are on either side of darkened
stage, singing "Plain We Live." Curtain lights up, and
behind barn we see* AMISH MEN *and* WOMEN *slowly
walking up ramp and exiting.* KATIE *is last one up
ramp. She stands for a moment looking toward* PETER,
*as he looks toward her. With last note of song, the
chorus slowly exits, and behind curtain* KATIE *slowly
walks off.* PETER *is left alone on stage, deserted and
shunned.*)

(AMISH *sing*)

Plain we live,
For plain we see
It's good for people to live plain.

Hard we work,
So life is good.
When life is hard we don't complain.

To our Amish way we must be true
For here we stay to keep the faith,

PLAIN AND FANCY

The faith our fathers knew.
Plain we live
For plain is good,
And plain is how we mean to stay.
To God we pray
To keep us plain!

Curtain

ACT TWO

ACT TWO

Scene I

A section of DAN's *farmland.*

There are some traces of the burned-down barn; a new barn is being erected by a group of AMISH MEN, *including* PAPA *and* EZRA. WOMEN *are bringing refreshments to the workers. The scene is busy and gay.*

>   (CHORUS *sings*)
>
>   How do you raise a barn?
>   How do you raise a barn?
>   You raise a barn with nails and wood.
>   With nails and wood and schwitzing good,
>   It comes a barn!
>   (DAN *enters.*)

DAN

Hello, Mr. Yoder. Where did all these people come from?

PAPA YODER

When we have a barn-raising, people come from all over to help.

DAN

You mean they all volunteer to work like this?

HILDA

By us a barn-raising means to help and enjoy!

DAN

You'll be at this for weeks.

PAPA YODER

Not us, Mr. King. Just wait and see!

(*He sings*)
How do you raise a barn?
How do you raise a barn?
You raise a barn with careful hands.
So strong it looks and strong it stands,
With careful hands so strong it stands,
With nails and wood and schwitzing good
It comes a barn.

How do you raise a barn?
How do you raise a barn?
You raise it with your neighbor
Who helps you with your labor,
Who works all day with careful hands,
With careful hands so strong it stands,
With nails and wood and schwitzing good
It comes a barn!

(*After barn is up*)
That's how you raise a barn!
With nails and wood
And schwitzing good
It comes a barn!

FIRST AMISH MAN
(*To* EZRA)
It'll be a better barn than was before!

EZRA

Yah. (*To* PAPA) Looks real solid, ain't?

PAPA YODER

The old barn was solid also.

FOURTH AMISH MAN
(*To* EZRA)
A terrible thing to happen just before your wedding.

ISAAC

Funny, Peter was always . . .

PAPA YODER

I want no talk of Peter! Let him stay shunned!
(*They go back to work, as* HILDA *enters, carrying
pitcher and glasses.*)

THIRD AMISH MAN
(*Calls*)
Hilda! You got something to drink? I'm busting from the
heat!

HILDA

Here . . .
(*Pours him drink.*)

THIRD AMISH MAN

Hilda . . . you want maybe to go with me later, over by the lake?

HILDA

No.

THIRD AMISH MAN

It will be cool sitzing by the lake.

HILDA

So go sitz.

THIRD AMISH MAN

Why don't you want to come with me?

HILDA

Because I don't want to.

THIRD AMISH MAN

Because why not?

HILDA

Because you're skinny!

THIRD AMISH MAN

(*Amazed*)

What's skinny got to do?

HILDA

Finish with the drink once!

PLAIN AND FANCY

THIRD AMISH MAN

Because I'm skinny just, you won't go?
(*Vigorously scratches his side.*)

HILDA

Also, you're all the time crotzing.
(*He stops scratching abruptly.*)

THIRD AMISH MAN

What's crotzing got to do?

HILDA

Give me the glass once.

THIRD AMISH MAN

Come with me by the lake!

HILDA

Leave me be. Find a girl who enjoys a skinny crotzer!

FOURTH AMISH MAN
(*Crosses to them; nudges his friend jocularly*)
It's no use, Jacob. This one likes *no* feller!

HILDA

Maybe.

FIFTH AMISH MAN

Maybe? You found a feller, Hilda?

HILDA

Maybe.

FOURTH AMISH MAN

Look how she looks! Not maybe! For sure!

THIRD AMISH MAN

So who is it once? Not fat. Not skinny. Not big. Not little. Not a crotzer. Not ferhoodled.

HILDA

Also not fershpritzed!
(*Pours glass of water on him and runs off laughing, almost bumping into* RUTH, *entering.* HILDA *exits.*)

RUTH

(*To* AMISH MAN)
There's a happy one.

FOURTH AMISH MAN

Sure. She found a fellow!

RUTH

Really? Who's the lucky boy?

JACOB YODER

We don't know who. Not any fellow from around here, for sure!

FOURTH AMISH MAN

Not one of us, for sure.

110

RUTH

(*Quizzically, looking after* HILDA, *then at* DAN)
He always did like buttermilk.

DAN

(*Seeing* RUTH *for first time*)
Ruth, you should have seen these people pitch in and work together . . . and did you taste this nut streusel? It's sensational. These people know how to live!

RUTH

Dan, why don't you buy a big black hat and move in?

DAN

Hilda made it.

RUTH

Oh!

DAN

That kid's a great cook!

RUTH

(*Testing him*)
Cute, too!

DAN

She sure is! And you know, she's very bright. . . .

RUTH

I know. We had a long talk about underwear.

111

DAN

And she's so honest. No pretenses. Just . . . just . . .

RUTH

Just plain folks! She's quite young though, isn't she?

DAN

No, she's twenty-two. She just has a very youthful quality.

RUTH

At twenty-two, what's the trick?

DAN

Who'd ever expect to find a girl like Hilda in this kind of place? (PAPA YODER *starts to cross downstage center*) I thought they'd all be much more . . .
(PETER *enters.* DAN *stops as he sees him.* MEN *abruptly stop talking and working, and turn from him.*)

PETER

(*Crosses to* PAPA YODER)
Mr. Yoder . . .

PAPA YODER

(*Turning from him; calling to* AMISH MAN)
David, you can start putting in the hay now!

PETER

Mr. Yoder, it was not a hex on the barn.
(*There is no response, all have their backs to him.*)

EZRA

(*To* AMISH MAN)

It is a nervy thing how a man who is shunned tries to talk to others.

AMISH MAN

It wouldn't wonder me if he had nerve even to come to your wedding.

EZRA

After fighting and hexing my farm, even.

PETER

(*To* EZRA)

It is not yet your farm.

EZRA

(*To* AMISH MEN)

Enough for now, ain't? Time to eat!
(*All exit right, passing* DAN *and* RUTH. PETER, *alone, defeated, starts off left.*)

DAN

Peter! (PETER *continues to exit*) Peter! (PETER *turns, and* DAN *goes to him*) Peter, I'm sorry. I feel somehow that I caused all this.

PETER

No, it was not you. I am leaving here.

DAN

Where are you going?

PETER

Some place. I do not know for sure yet.

DAN

If there's anything at all I can do . . .

PETER

Maybe the farm . . . if I had that . . . (*Breaks off*) No,
you were right. It would not help.
> (KATIE *enters, carrying basket to collect pitcher and
> glasses.*)

KATIE

(*Sees* PETER. *They look at each other for a moment, then she
deliberately turns her back on him. Then speaks*)
Lunch is ready, Mr. King!

DAN

Peter is leaving, Katie.
> (*She doesn't answer.*)

PETER

Katie, come with me.
> (*She turns to him, turns away.*)

KATIE

(*To* DAN)
I must not talk to him, Mr. King. He is shunned.

DAN

But Katie . . .

KATIE

(*Sharply, very hurt*)
I am yet Amish, Mr. King! He is shunned.
(DAN *looks at* KATIE *and* PETER, *slowly exits right with*
RUTH.)

PETER

Katie, you want to come with me, and you know you do.
. . . Katie, listen . . . listen once . . . if not to me . . . to
your own self.

(*He sings*)

Follow your heart
Whenever it calls to you,
Whatever it tells you to do.
The heart has reasons
The mind can not know.
Follow your heart
Wherever it wants you to go.

Lost in the night,
You wonder what path to take
'Til a whisper comes through,
Come out of the darkness
Into the day.
Your heart knows the way.
Follow your heart

To the someone who needs you
As he did from the start,

To the someone who waits for you
To follow your heart.

> (*During the number* HILDA *comes on from left, and hears* PETER *sing the last few bars to* KATIE.)

PETER

Katie . . .

> (*She runs left and is confronted by* HILDA. PETER *is obscured from view by curtain closing.* HILDA *and* KATIE *remain in view in front of curtain.*

KATIE

> (*Going to* HILDA)

I must not listen to him, ain't? . . . I'm doing right, ain't, Hilda?

HILDA

I do not know for sure. I feel only one thing. . . .

> (HILDA *and* KATIE *sing "Follow Your Heart."*)

Scene II

Kitchen of the Yoder home with old-fashioned wood-burning cooking range, a sink with water pump, a butter churn, corner cupboard, tables crowded with pots, pans, etc.

EMMA and FIVE AMISH WOMEN are bustling about, cooking, stirring, slicing, etc.

BESSIE

(At stove, taking out tray)
Streusel Kuchen I think we'll have enough, Emma.

EMMA

You think?

BESSIE

Plenty. Ninety-two people you counted for the wedding, ain't, Emma?

EMMA

(Grinding meat at table, center)
Yah!

REBECCA

I heard Abraham Lapp and his cousins can't come.
(She is rolling Shupp Noodles at table, right.)

EMMA

Oh! Then figure eighty-six.

RACHEL

(*Who is churning butter*)
Don't forget Rebecca Mast and the kids.

EMMA

All right, ninety-one. The babies, too?

RACHEL

Sure!

EMMA

Ninety-five! Make already for one hundred. What they don't fress up, we'll give to the pigs.

BESSIE

(*Crossing to pump to wash hands*)
Yah, Emma.

REBECCA

Esther, see if the sauerkraut ain't finished.
(ESTHER *goes to stove.* RUTH *enters, surveys the scene.*)

SARAH

(*Tasting*)
Needs more salt, the shmeer-kase.

EMMA

Yah, yah!

REBECCA

(*Crossing to center table for spoon*)
Needs more water the dough!

118

ESTHER

(Crossing up center for salt, then back to stove)
The sauerkraut's coming good!

EMMA

Good, good.
(Girl enters, carrying huge side of raw beef, passes
RUTH *and takes it to center table.)*

RUTH

(Indicates beef)
Looks like he had a bad night.

EMMA

(Looks up)
Hello, Miss Winters!

RUTH

I heard there's a bit of cooking going on. I'd like to help.
(She tries to keep out of the way of the bustling women.)

EMMA

You want to help cook?

RUTH

Sure. What was that dish Mr. King enjoyed so much at lunch . . . shnitzel-something . . . ?

EMMA

Kassel-Ripschen.

RUTH

That's it. How do you make it?

EMMA

Oh, I can't show you now, we're so busy fixing for the wedding.

RUTH

Well, let me help . . . maybe I can pick up a few pointers.

EMMA

Sure, then.

ESTHER

Miss please . . . if you can fill this pail with water from the pump . . .

RUTH

Glad to! (*Takes pail and starts pumping*) Nothing's coming out.

EMMA

Pump, pump! It'll come out water.

RUTH

(*To* RACHEL, *who is churning next to her*)
I'd love to get one of these where it comes out Scotch. (RACHEL *gives her a cold stare.* RUTH *continues pumping. Water starts coming out*) Hey, it works! This is fun.

SARAH

Miss, there, on the stove, in the big pot, the water is boiling?

RUTH
(*Stops pumping, goes to stove*)
Yes, it is. . . .

SARAH
It's for rice. So put in please, from the box rice.

RUTH
(*Starts pouring rice, carefully*)
Happy to!

ESTHER
The pail is filled already once?

RUTH
Just a minute. I'm new at this.

EMMA
So pump, please. We need it quick!

RUTH
Okay!
(*Pours in whole box of rice . . . then leisurely crosses to pump.*)

EMMA
(*Impatiently*)
Pump, pump!
(RUTH *hurries to the pump and starts to work.*)

RACHEL

Ooh, I'm tired so!

RUTH

What's that you're doing?

RACHEL

Churning butter . . . for two hours yet!

RUTH

You must be exhausted. Let me do it. . . .

RACHEL

Thank you.
(*She busies herself elsewhere, as* RUTH *starts churning.*)

ESTHER

(*Calls to her*)
The pail of water, I need it for the potatoes!

RUTH

So sorry!
(*Starts pumping and churning simultaneously.*)

BESSIE

(*On her way to the cupboard with cakes*)
It's fun cooking by us, ain't?

RUTH

This is more sport than basket-weaving! (*She churns and pumps. Suddenly she notices that the rice has risen a few inches above the pot*) Er . . . miss . . . madam . . . the pot there!

> (*The women are too busy to notice her. . . .* RUTH *quickly crosses, picks up lid and firmly puts it down on pot, pushing rice down.*)

RACHEL

The butter ain't finished yet, miss!

RUTH

Oh, the butter!
> (*Starts churning again.*)

ESTHER

Miss, the water, please!

RUTH

In a second!
> (*Starts pumping as well as churning.*)

REBECCA

Emma, help me with the shupp-noodles!

EMMA

Wait once! I'm grinding for knockwurst!

123

REBECCA

First help grease the pan here!

EMMA

Oh, all right then. . . . (*To* RUTH *over her shoulder*) Miss, please, grind up please the last few pieces. If you're not busy.

RUTH

My pleasure!
(*Starts to grind meat, then pumps, then churns, notices rice which has risen again. She hastily crosses to the stove and slams the lid down on the pot. The women who are oblivious of* RUTH's *dilemma, continue their work and conversation.*)

SARAH

Taste for me the shmeer-kase.

EMMA

Don't put too much salt.

BESSIE

(*Who is at cupboard*)
Rebecca Mast is bringing more dishes?

EMMA

Yah!
(*Meanwhile* RUTH *has gone to grinding and churning, churning and pumping water. She sees that the rice has risen again and starts for the stove.* EMMA *is com-*

ing down to the center table for more ground meat and substitutes an empty plate. She almost bumps into RUTH *who is looking very sheepish at this point.*)

EMMA

(*Stopping* RUTH *and motioning her to go back to the pump*)
Pump, pump!
(RUTH *goes back to churning and pumping water. As soon as* EMMA *is busy again at the center table,* RUTH *dashes to the stove and this time slams down an old-fashioned flatiron on the lid. Feeling quite satisfied this time that the matter is taken care of once and for all, she nonchalantly starts back to the pump.*)

ESTHER

(*To* RUTH, *impatiently*)
The water, please!

RUTH

(*Pumping*)
Coming!

RACHEL

The butter is made yet?

RUTH

(*Churning*)
In a jiffy!

EMMA

The liver, miss!

RUTH
(*Grinding*)

I'm with you! (REBECCA *has gone to the stove to look at the sauerkraut, notices the rice cascading out of the pot and lets out a loud gasp.* WOMEN *all look toward the stove and then stare at* RUTH *accusingly. After pause, with phony calm*) You'll have to excuse me, ladies, I'm late for an appointment with a hatbox!
(*She exits.*)

SARAH
(*Going back to the churn*)

The lady from New York, she ain't acquainted so good by the kitchen.

REBECCA
(*Cleaning up the mess at the stove*)

But who cooks by her in the house? The husband?

BESSIE

She ain't got a husband.

EMMA

No wonder, the way she cooks. Bessie, go by the cellar and bring salt.

BESSIE

Yah, Emma.
(*She exits.*)

EMMA

You see how it is with a city lady? Ach, they have such a sad life.

126

PLAIN AND FANCY

RACHEL

Maybe if we was city ladies, we would enjoy there?

EMMA

Enjoy? No, never!

(EMMA *sings*)

Once upon a time there was a country mouse
Paid a visit to her relative, the city mouse,
But she didn't care a bit for her city house
And her heart was full of pity for the city mouse.
I felt the same as she,
A city mouse I'd never want to be. . . .

City mouse, city mouse, full of care,
What dress to buy? What dress to wear?
Country mouse, country mouse, worries not,
She wears the only one she's got.

City mouse, city mouse, fuss and fret

(FIRST AMISH GIRL *sings*)

What should she be—blond or brunette?

(EMMA *sings*)

Country mouse reckons a diff'rent way,
She's happy if it don't turn gray.

(AMISH WOMAN *sings*)

The city mouse must always watch her figure,

(EMMA *sings*)

She better keep it slender if she's wise.
It's diff'rent with the fellers in the country,
They like the large, economy size.

(SECOND AMISH GIRL *sings*)

City mouse wonders what love's about,

(GIRLS *sing*)

She reads a book to puzzle it out.

(EMMA *sings*)

Country mouse, country mouse reads no book,
She goes into the barn and takes a look.

(EMMA *sings*)

City mouse tries to be brainy kind,
Wants to be loved just for her mind.
Country mouse, country mouse, well aware,
What fellers want is not up there.
    (*Taps forehead*)

(THIRD AMISH GIRL *sings*)

City mouse mother in such a stew,
Raising one child so hard to do.

(EMMA *sings*)

Country mouse, country mouse, she does fine,
Number one takes care of number nine.

(AMISH WOMAN *sings*)

No complicated gadgets in the kitchen,

PLAIN AND FANCY

(THIRD GIRL *sings*)

No complicated notions in the head,

(EMMA *sings*)

And when it's time for maybe getting married
No complications in the bed.

(THIRD GIRL *sings*)

City mouse, city mouse, one fine day,
Pack up your bag, tiptoe away.

(EMMA *sings*)

Look around till you've found a country spouse

(ENSEMBLE *sings*)

And settle down to be a country mouse!

Scene III

Back porch of the Yoder home. DAN, PAPA YODER *and* ISAAC.

PAPA YODER
I tell you, mister, forty-five hundred is a fair price.

ISAAC
Yah . . . is a good price.

DAN
To tell you the truth, Mr. Yoder, someone else is interested in the property.

PAPA YODER
For real?

DAN
Yes.

PAPA YODER
(Pause)
Forty-*eight* hundred.

ISAAC
Is a good price.

DAN
I'll have to talk to this other person before I decide.

PAPA YODER
An Amish man?

130

DAN

Yes.

PAPA YODER

Five thousand.

ISAAC

Is a *good* price.

DAN

Mr. Yoder, I want to hear what this other fellow offers.

PAPA YODER

What other fellow?

DAN

Peter.

PAPA YODER

(*Angrily*)

Peter! Mister, this is shrecklich! A hexer, a sinful person,
he wants only to hurt me with this talk of buying your farm!

DAN

He doesn't want to hurt you, Mr. Yoder. The barn was no
more hexed than . . .

PAPA YODER

(*Interrupts*)

You want to sell your place, or no?

131

DAN

I think you're being unfair to the boy. All I'm trying to do . . .

PAPA YODER

Don't try! Katie is going to marry Ezra! Don't try nothing!

DAN

(*Pause, looks at* PAPA YODER *deliberately*)
Mr. Yoder, I had another offer for the land. For a good deal more money. I didn't consider it because I thought it would hurt you people. But maybe I was wrong.

ISAAC

Hurt how, mister?

DAN

This company wants to build a factory here.

PAPA YODER

A factory?

DAN

A paper-box factory. There would be over a thousand workers, I imagine.

ISAAC

City people!

DAN

I thought it would be unfair to your community. But you don't hesitate to be unfair, even to one of your own.

132

PAPA YODER
(*Pauses, furiously*)
Do it then! Sell it to them! Bring in the strangers! Me you
can't handle like this!
(*Starts to exit.* ISAAC *holds him back.*)

ISAAC
Jacob! Think once! Think what happened in Stultville.
Bird-in-Hand will not be for us any more.

PAPA YODER
Then we will go!

ISAAC
Jacob! Your pride is worth more than everything?
(PAPA JACOB YODER *looks at* DAN *bitterly. Exits.*)

ISAAC
Mister, such a thing you could not do.

DAN
I don't want to hurt any of you. But I do want to help a boy
who's in trouble.
(HILDA *enters.*)

HILDA
Papa, in the kitchen Mama wants you!

ISAAC
(*Preoccupied*)
What?

133

HILDA

In the stove, the fire needs fixing.

ISAAC

All right. Mister, you'll think on it, ain't?

DAN

I will. But I hope Mr. Yoder does some thinking, too.

ISAAC

Yah.
(*Exits.*)

HILDA

I'm happy you and Papa are friendly-like.

DAN

He seems like a very nice man.

HILDA

Yah. We are all friendly here.

DAN

Are you?

HILDA

Oh, sure. From us Amish came bundling.

DAN

You can't get much friendlier than that!

134

HILDA

(*Smiles at him . . . Pause*)

Dan . . .

DAN

Yes?

HILDA

I was happy like anything when you said I was a pretty one, and all like that.

DAN

Well, I meant it, Hilda. Every word of it.

HILDA

I know you did. I felt for sure you were not like making fun with me.

DAN

Of course not.

HILDA

Your grandfather was Amish, ain't?

DAN

Sure. Old Joshua Koenig.

HILDA

Koenig. I like the sound of it. Koenig.

DAN

It's King now. That's what it means, you know.

HILDA

I know. It fits you. It's strong-like. I like you very much, Dan. More than any man around here, ever.

DAN

I like you too, Hilda.

HILDA

You do?

DAN

Very much.

HILDA

Oh, Papa will be surprised to hear!

DAN

To hear what?

HILDA

He said always I am not for marrying.

DAN

Marrying . . . ?

HILDA

(*Happily*)

Oh, when Papa hears your name is really Koenig!

DAN

(*Stops her*)

Hilda!

136

HILDA

(*Sincerely*)

I will make you a good wife, Dan. Surely.

DAN

Hilda . . . sit down.

HILDA

I am sitting.

DAN

Oh, yes. Of course. Hilda, you're an Amish girl. I'm a New Yorker. You could only be happy here.

HILDA

I could be happy any place, I think.

DAN

Hilda, please listen to me. . . .

HILDA

Yes, Dan . . .

DAN

I said I like you. I do like you. Very much. You're a **fine** girl, a wonderful girl. But . . . that's all I meant, really.

HILDA

(*Puzzled and hurt*)

You do not want marrying?

137

DAN

Hilda, it's impossible. Believe me, it wouldn't be fair to you.

HILDA

(*Realizes*)

You do not want marrying.

DAN

Listen to me. You don't know me. You don't know how I live. You don't really know what it would be like to be away from here. Do you understand me?

HILDA

I understand only one thing clear. You do not want marrying.

DAN

Can't you see how wrong it is, Hilda? You'd be lost away from here. We're as far apart as . . . as Bird-in-Hand is from New York. I'm going back there in a day or two. . . . (HILDA *sits quietly, looks at him for a moment; then abruptly rises and runs off*) Now, wait, Hilda!

(DAN *throws cigarette down and stamps on it, furious with himself. Starts to exit. Landscape curtain closes.* GIRLS *pass him.*)

FIRST GIRL

(*As* DAN *exits—disregarding them*)

Hello, Mr. King! That's him. . . . That's the one Hilda's stuck on.

138

SECOND GIRL

Him?

THIRD GIRL

But he's not Amish even!

SECOND GIRL

That Hilda!

THIRD GIRL

She's getting to be a terrible wild one!

FIRST GIRL

Should we tell her Papa?

THIRD GIRL

No.

SECOND GIRL

We ought to tell somebody!

FIRST GIRL

Who?

SECOND GIRL

Let's tell all the other girls!
    (*All exit.*)

Scene IV

RUTH's *room.*
RUTH *is at the bed, frantically trying to get her hatbox open.*

RUTH

I never needed a drink this bad! (*She claws at the lock with her nails*) Torn to shreds in an Amish kitchen! He's not worth it. Ouch! (*Waves her finger in pain. She takes off a shoe and starts hacking at the lock. She stops, throws shoe down, pants heavily and stares at hatbox*) That dandy Mark Cross and his dandy guaranteed locks! (*She goes to the dresser looking for the key*) That key must be here someplace! (*She discovers a nail file and decides to try that. She pries at the lock, and bends the nail file into a horseshoe. She flings it on the bed*) It's the booze hex, that's what it is! I've got to get this thing open. . . . (*Crosses to window, leans out*) You, there . . . yoo . . . hoo . . . could you come up a minute? I need some help!

> (*She lights a cigarette, and is putting on her shoe when there is a knock.* EZRA *enters. He stares at her cigarette.*)

RUTH

Oh . . . this. Well, I'm a Baptist and we're allowed! Ezra, could you give me a hand? See if you can get this hatbox open.

146

EZRA

I'll try, anyway. (*He tugs at the lock, then turns to* RUTH)
It's stuck.

RUTH

I know, dear. That's the problem.

EZRA

Let me try again.
> (EZRA *picks up the hatbox, pulls at it with great effort.*
> *The top of the hatbox flies open and the lock flies*
> *off.*)

RUTH

You *are* a sturdy one! Thanks a lot. Er . . . sit down.
(EZRA *hesitates. She goes to the hatbox and gets a bottle of*
Scotch, starts to cross to dresser for glass. Notices EZRA *still*
standing) Have a sitz! (EZRA *does so. . . . She notices him*
staring while she pours herself a drink) Oh, we Baptists are
a wild bunch! (*Then in toast*) Gesundheit! (*Drinks. Sits on*
chest at foot of bed) Say, you do have muscles, don't you?

EZRA
(*Smiling*)
I am maybe the strongest one around.

RUTH

Congratulations!

EZRA
(*Staring at her drink*)
What is that?

RUTH

Well . . . er . . . it's a tonic . . . sort of.

141

EZRA

For women's troubles?

RUTH

For women's troubles, men's troubles . . . anybody's troubles. It's made out of er . . . er . . . vegetables.

EZRA

Vegetables . . . ?

RUTH

Sure . . . corn and rye and barley, stuff like that. Very good for the nerves.

EZRA

Oh! Well . . . today also I am a little nervous. With the barn burning, and my wedding tomorrow . . . and . . .
(*He reaches for the glass.*)

RUTH

Oh, no! You're not that nervous! Let's just talk a little.

EZRA

Talk?

RUTH

Yes . . . Well, Ezra, you're getting married tomorrow . . . ?

EZRA

Yah. . . . Maybe, could I taste the vegetable juice?
(*Taking glass from* RUTH.)

RUTH

Well . . .

EZRA

(*Sniffing drink. Incredulous*)
Vegetables?

RUTH

That's right!

EZRA

(*Slugs down drink, exhales deeply, still can't believe it*)
Vegetables?

RUTH

Well . . . ah . . . *old* vegetables! Now, we can talk.

EZRA

(*With a broad grin*)
Yah!

RUTH

Yah! I don't suppose you'd care for a cigarette, would you?

EZRA

Oh, no, no . . . Cigarettes are forbidden.
(*Takes bottle and pours drink.*)

RUTH

Now, wait a minute!

EZRA

(*About to drink, stops and toasts*)
Gezundheit!

RUTH

That's your opinion!
(EZRA *slugs down the drink: it seems to have no effect.*)

EZRA

Now we talk!

RUTH

What do you want to talk about?

EZRA

Yah!

RUTH

You said it! Well, now! Ezra, what kind of crops do you raise mainly?

EZRA

Crops?

RUTH

Yes. (EZRA *giggles*) I guess I shouldn't have asked that, I barely know you. (*Both start to reach for bottle,* EZRA *beats her to it*) Go ahead! Don't be shy!
(*He downs the drink.* RUTH *takes bottle away and puts it on dresser.*)

EZRA

(In sudden loud voice)
My Uncle Albert died funny!

RUTH

What?

EZRA

He was plowing by the turnips, he came home for supper,
all of a sudden he breathed hard-like and then died-like!

RUTH

(Stares at him)
That reminds *me* of a funny one! I have a little cousin . . .
(EZRA *roars with laughter*) You said it! (*There is a knock at
the door*) Oh, my God! You can't be found here! You better
get out of sight. . . . Come here. . . . (*She pulls him
toward curtained-off section of the room, pushing him behind
it. There is another knock*) Just a minute. . . . Coming!
(EZRA *stands grinning over the top of the curtain. Another
knock at the door*) Just a minute! (RUTH *pushes* EZRA *down to
a sitting position on floor, obscured by curtain*) Down boy!
(*Another knock.* RUTH *becomes aware that* EZRA's *feet are protruding from beneath the curtain.* RUTH *laboriously pushes at*
EZRA's *feet in an effort to conceal them*) Who is it?

HILDA

(From outside the door, answering)
Hilda!

RUTH

(*Still trying to conceal* EZRA's *shoes*)
Oh! What do you want, Hilda?

HILDA

(*Entering*)
I want to see you a minute. . . .

RUTH

(*Aware that* HILDA *has seen* EZRA's *protruding feet*)
Er . . . My walking shoes . . .

HILDA

Miss Ruth, I want you should give me a cigarette!

RUTH

Sure, dear. I . . . what?

HILDA

I want to smoke and all! Like you!

RUTH

This whole community is falling apart! What's the matter,
honey?

HILDA

(*Tearfully*)
What's the good to be Amish? I want to be like you and
him.

RUTH

Who? . . . Oh, you mean Dan?

146

HILDA

He is not for marrying a one like me. He said so!

RUTH

Marrying?

HILDA

I thought for sure he liked me. He said I was so pretty and all. And now . . . (*As she paces the room, she notices* EZRA's *shoes sticking out. Goes over and pulls back curtain*) Ezra! What are you doing there?

EZRA

Sitzing.

HILDA

Why are you sitzing?

EZRA

I'm tired.

HILDA
(*Sniffing*)
Ezra . . . you're drinking shnapps!

EZRA
(*With happy smile*)
From vegetables!

HILDA
(*To* RUTH)
What happened to him?

RUTH

Well, sir! We were sitting around telling funny stories . . .

HILDA

Ezra? He was never for fun.

EZRA

Now, I'm for fun! You know what? Over by Lancaster, there is a carnival.

HILDA

So?

EZRA

So I'm going!

HILDA

Ezra! A carnival? With music and nokkid girls and gambling games? An Amish to go to such a place?

EZRA

(*Gleefully*)

Once!

RUTH

Ezra! You're getting married tomorrow and . . .

EZRA

So I'm going! Today! Anybody wants to come with? Hilda . . . ?

148

HILDA

(*Indicating she is considering it*)
To the carnival?

RUTH

Hilda? She can't go to a place like that! An Amish girl!
What's the matter with you?

EZRA

So nobody's going? So good-bye, I'll come back later,
when I'm here sometime.
(*Lurches out.*)

RUTH

Wait a minute, Ezra!
(*She exits.*)

HILDA

To the carnival?

(*She sings; during the song, she takes off her blouse
and skirt, puts on RUTH's brassière over her own
chemise, then puts on RUTH's bright red dress and fur
piece.*)

Maybe he thinks I'm sitting in a corner,
Sobbing like a ninny
With my eyes all red.
Or maybe he thinks I'm standing in the garden
Staring at his window,
Wishing I was dead.
Well, he can just go and soak his head!

I'll show him!
I'll show him how little I care,
When we meet I'll just stand with my nose in the air!
Though he's sighing,
And pleading and down on his knees,
I'll tell him I think he's full of cheese!

He can just save his breath,
He can leave me alone.
If he's starving to death,
I won't throw him a bone.

I'll show him!
How happy I am to be free
Of a nothing who's nothing to me!

He'll find out I'm not yet such a baby,
I'm all through with acting like a dunce.
Any girl who thinks he's worth the having
Ought to have her head examined once.
He's too old for me—he must be fifty,
Any feller fifty is no prize.
Furthermore, his eyes are kind of shifty,
I don't trust a man with shifty eyes!

I'll show him how easy he is to forget.
In a week I won't even remember him, yet
I'll be flirting with fellers I don't even know
In . . . wherever it is fellers go.

Fancy dresses I'll wear
Fancy pants underneath,

PLAIN AND FANCY

Fine perfume in my hair
And a rose in my teeth.
I'll show him!—the way he showed me—
What a smart girl a lummox can be!

Me he won't find sitting home and moping,
I'll go places where I've never been.
Papa says by Lancaster is sinful,
I'll go down to Lancaster and sin!
    (*She exits.*)

Scene V

A section of the road before the landscape curtain.
PETER *sitting on bench.* TWO AMISH BOYS *pass* PETER *and deliberately ignore him.* KATIE *enters.*)

PETER

(*Rising*)
Katie, you should not have come by my house. Somebody will see you.

KATIE

I know it is wrong, but I could not help it. Only to say good-bye I came. Maybe I will not see you again ever.

PETER

No, Katie. You will not see me again. Ever.

KATIE

Peter, my heart is hurt by your shunning. For loving me only you suffer. (PETER *turns away from her*) Also, for loving you, I suffer. . . .

PETER

Good-bye, Katie. . . .
(RUTH *enters.*)

152

RUTH

Peter, where's Ezra?

PETER

I have not seen him.

RUTH

Oh, fine! He really went to that Carnival!

KATIE

Carnival? Ezra went to the carnival? He must be fericht.

RUTH

He's also a little plastered . . . drunk. You ought to get
him home, Peter.

PETER

Let Katie's Papa bring him home.

RUTH

I hope nothing happens to him . . . the day before his
wedding. It would be quite a scandal, wouldn't it?

PETER

Yah . . .
    (*Doesn't move.*)

RUTH

Maybe I can find Dan somewhere. . . .

153

PETER

(*Looks at* KATIE)

I will go!

KATIE

Peter, it could bring you more trouble!

PETER

He is yet my brother. And shame he must not bring on you!

KATIE

(*Stepping toward him*)

Peter . . . you will come back?

PETER

No, not ever. I will send Ezra back.

(*Exits left.*)

RUTH

Katie . . . Katie, it's getting cool, why don't you come into the house with me?

KATIE

No, thank you. I will maybe stay here, and wait . . . a little.

(RUTH *exits*)

(KATIE *sings*)

. . . Soon enough the carefree days,
The sunlit days go by,
Soon enough the bluebird has to fly.
We were foolish,

PLAIN AND FANCY

One day we fell in love.
Now we wonder
What we were dreaming of,
Smiling in the sunlight, laughing in the rain,
I wish that we were young and foolish again.

(*Lights fade*)

SCENE VI

Midway of the Carnival grounds in Lancaster.
Crowds on stage crossing, couples flirting, others listening
to the Barker's spiel.

BARKER

All right, folks . . . step right up! See the ninth wonder
of the world . . . Madame Zanda, the human pincushion!
Right here, only a dime! Step right up folks!

EZRA

(Wandering in with the crowd, going to a "sharpie")
Hey, mister, where do they sell here vegetable juice?
(The man ignores him, and EZRA goes into the dance
hall.)

BARKER

Only a dime, folks! Step right in and see **Madame Zanda,**
the human pincushion!

A GIRL

I don't think it's possible to stick pins in a woman!

SAILOR

I'll take two!
(Musical introduction and Carnival ballet. During the
ballet, HILDA enters. She is accosted by a masher. EZRA

156

drunkenly tries to help her, starting a brawl. PETER, *who has come here looking for* EZRA, *succeeds in getting him out of the dance hall.* HILDA *and* EZRA *leave.* PETER *is in the center of a free-for-all fight, and as it rises to its height, the curtain comes down.)*

Scene VII

A section of the road before the landscape curtain. Time is after the Carnival. EZRA *comes staggering on.* RACHEL *and an* AMISH GIRL *pass and give* EZRA *a reproachful look. Two more* AMISH GIRLS *pass and give* EZRA *a look and then titter and run off. The young* MILLER CHILDREN *enter. Soft music is heard throughout entire scene.*

MILLER BOY
(Stopping him, bellows)
Ezra!
*(*EZRA *clutches his head as if struck, continues to stagger on his way with the* MILLER CHILDREN *preceding him. The lights fade.)*

Scene VIII

Back porch of the Yoder home. RUTH *appears with a pan of Schnitz und Knepp which she has just cooked. She places it on a bench and takes off her apron. She starts to pace, looking off in both directions.*

DAN
(Entering)

Any sign of them?

RUTH

No.

DAN

I told you to leave that bottle in the car.

RUTH

I didn't force it on him. He was nervous.

DAN

If Papa Yoder finds out about this Amish delegation to a carnival . . .

RUTH

He knows. . . . I told him.

DAN

You told him? What did you do that for?

159

RUTH

Why not? Let him know that Peter went there to help his brother! After what he did to the poor kid. Let him think about it a little!

DAN

What did he say?

RUTH

He stared at me for a few minutes and I left.

DAN

(*Looks off*)

Still no sign of them. (*Absently tastes from dish*) Mmmmm . . . taste this!

RUTH

I did.

DAN

Kassel Ripschen.

RUTH

Schnitz und Knepp.

DAN

It's wonderful.

RUTH

Horrible.

DAN

These apples are mashed or shredded or something.

160

RUTH

No, first you dice them and then you . . .
(She stops.)

DAN

(Looks at her)

Then you what?

RUTH

Forget it!

DAN

Ruth! You made this Kassel Ripschen!!

RUTH

Schnitz und Knepp! They've been gone an awfully long
time.

DAN

Why did you make this, Ruth?

RUTH

Do me a favor and forget it. I apologize.

DAN

You made it because you knew I liked it.

RUTH

No, I didn't. Don't be maudlin.

DAN

I think you did.

RUTH

(*Bursts out*)

All right, I made it because you liked it!

DAN

Ruth!

RUTH

And if you want to know why I went skiing with you last winter and almost broke my back, it's because *you* were on a skiing binge! And that damn duck-hunting kick you were on —I almost froze standing up to my elbows in that miserable swamp!

DAN

Honey!

RUTH

Well, here's your beloved Schnitz und Knepp . . . and when you go in for parachute-jumping, you jump alone!

DAN

(*Holds her back*)

Ruth!

RUTH

Oh, get away from me!

DAN

I never realized that . . . it just never occurred to me that . . . you really made this?

162

RUTH

Oh, you're a boob!

DAN

I guess I am. (*Looks at her*) I mean, I was.
 (*He draws her to him, they kiss.*)

RUTH

And every year I'll make Schnitz und Knepp for you . . .
on Eric von Stroheim's birthday. What about Hilda?

DAN

Oh . . . yes.

RUTH

What are you going to do about it, Dan?

DAN

I don't know. I was just being friendly and . . .

RUTH

I know, I know.

DAN

I still don't know what happened. She met someone wearing a collar and tie, and . . . I don't know *what* happened.

RUTH

Dan, you'll have to talk to her.

DAN

I tried! But what will I tell her? Maybe we can . . .

163

RUTH

(*As* HILDA *enters*)

You, Dan. I don't wear a collar and tie.

DAN

Hilda! What happened to you?

HILDA

(*Chastened*)

I was by the carnival.

DAN

What made you do that? (HILDA *doesn't answer*) Hilda, that was very foolish.

HILDA

No. I wanted to see different people than I live with always. And I *saw*. They made me afraid.

DAN

I'm sorry, Hilda.

HILDA

I do not know these people . . . just like you said. I do not know you even.

DAN

That's right.

HILDA

Coming back, I asked myself . . . who are these people? Who is this Dan? Neat he is and polite, and with shiny shoes. But a girl does not marry shiny shoes, ain't?

164

DAN

Of course not.

HILDA

Different he is from the men around here, but is he better?
(*To* DAN) Excuse me, *that* I don't know.

DAN

Of course. And there must be some very nice men here.

HILDA

Surely. And younger too. So I will look and I will find
him, ain't?
(*During song, curtain closes*)

(RUTH *sings*)
While looking around for that fortunate man,
One little word of warning from Aunt Ruth . . .

(DAN *sings*)
And Uncle Dan.

(RUTH *sings*)
Take your time and take your pick
Till you find the one designed to be your pick.

(DAN *sings*)
Never trust that first impression when a feller comes to call.

(RUTH *sings*)
As a matter of fact you're wiser never trusting him at all.

165

(DAN *sings*)

Look around before you leap
Though the ways of modern scientists are deep

(RUTH *sings*)

They ain't found a way to tell a good man from a creep,

(BOTH *sing*)

So take your time and take your pick.

(HILDA *sings*)

I'll take my time and take my pick
Till I'm sure beyond all cure that he's my pick.
He'll be handy in the barnyard with the cattle and the
sheep,

(RUTH *sings*)

He'll be handy on the sofa when the sheep have gone to
sleep,

(DAN *sings*)

But though his build seems early Greek,

(RUTH *sings*)

Though his monumental shoulders turn you weak,

(DAN *sings*)

Is it nature or the tailor gave him that physique?

(RUTH *sings*)

Take your time . . . and take a peek!

PLAIN AND FANCY

(DAN *sings*)

Take your time and take your pick.
Pick too quick and what a pickle you can pick.

(RUTH *sings*)

There's the kind of man who dazzles you with conversation bright,
Then you marry the guy and all he says is: "What's to eat
tonight?"

(DAN *sings*)

So take your time and time your pick,

(RUTH *sings*)

Don't just marry any Harry, Tom or Dick.

(DAN *sings*)

You can end up with no paddle up that famous creek.
So take your time and take your pick.

(HILDA *sings*)

I'll take my time and take my pick
Till I pick the one who'll stick through thin and thick.
At a party he won't notice when the pretty girls arrive.

(RUTH *sings*)

If you ever find a man like that, make sure he's still alive.

(DAN *sings*)

So take your time,

(RUTH *sings*)

Not too much time,
Don't delay until you're way beyond your prime.
They won't let you be so picky when you're old as I'm

(BOTH *sing*)

But take your time and take your pick. . . .

(DAN *sings*)

Till you find the one it's fun to dance with chick-to-chick,

(RUTH *sings*)

Who will never spike the shoofly pie with arsenic.

(HILDA *sings*)

I'll just look and look until I find the perfect . . . Zook!

(ALL THREE *sing*)

Take your time and take your pick.

Scene IX

The Yoder yard. The bird curtain opens. The MILLER CHILDREN *are seen dashing across the yard and into the house.*

MILLER CHILDREN

Uncle Jacob . . . Uncle Jacob!
 (EZRA *staggers on, disheveled.*)

RUTH

Look what's coming by the road over once!

DAN

(*Going to him*)
Ezra, what happened?

HILDA

If Uncle Jacob knows he was by the Carnival, it will be terrible around here!

DAN

Let's get him cleaned up a little!

KATIE

(*Entering*)
Ezra! Where is Peter?

EZRA

(*Vaguely*)
He was going someplace, I think.
 (PAPA YODER *and* KIDS *enter.*)

169

PAPA YODER

Ezra! You was at the Carnival!

EZRA

It was not plain vegetable juice.

PAPA YODER

You sinned like this?

EZRA

But I didn't start the fighting. . . .

PAPA YODER

Fighting also! The day before your wedding! And drunk yet! Look at you! Fighting and drinking in an evil place.

EZRA

I will be all right for the wedding.

PAPA YODER

There will be no wedding! My girl will not marry such a one!

EZRA

But my whole family is coming!

PAPA YODER

Everybody is coming, but I will have to send them away. Such a shame I never had yet. (*To* CHILDREN) Go into the house, children.

(*Enter* PETER *and* STATE TROOPER.)

KATIE

Peter!

HILDA

A policeman yet!

DAN

What's the trouble, Officer?

COP

This fellow was creating a disturbance at the Carnival.

DAN

Now look, Officer . . .

COP

I would have taken him in, only I figured I'd give him a break this one time.

PAPA YODER

Why did you bring him here like this?

COP

Look, mister, we never had any trouble with any of you people before, but this was a real brawl. . . . There were five guys laid out cold.

DAN

But he didn't start it, did he?

COP

I don't care who started it . . . he did his share. And he didn't even want to come back. I had to drag him.

PETER

(*Looks at* KATIE)

No, I did not want to come back.

COP

One more word out of you, and I will take you in.

PAPA YODER

For what, mister?

COP

For what? For creating a disturbance, like I said. What was he doing at a place like that anyway?

DAN

He didn't go there to make trouble, Officer.

PAPA YODER

I heard why he went. I been thinking why he went.

COP

He had no business being there.

PAPA YODER

He went by that place to help his brother only. His brother was making trouble, not him! To save his brother from shame he went there. To save us all from shame.

COP

Look, all I know is . . .

172

PAPA YODER

Know better that sometimes people punish too fast without thinking a little. It was a hard thing Peter did . . . and a good thing!

COP

Well as long as he behaves himself . . .
(*Exiting.*)

DAN

Everything will be all right, Officer. Thanks a lot!

PETER

Mister Yoder . . . Everybody is coming to a wedding to your house. . . . You should have a wedding for them, ain't?

KATIE

(*Crosses to* PETER)
Always we have wanted marrying, Papa.

DAN

They only want what you want, Mr. Yoder. A good Amish marriage and a good Amish family. Besides, Peter's a man of property. I'm selling him the river farm.

PAPA YODER

Katie, I always wanted what is good for you.

KATIE

I know, Papa.

PAPA YODER

Maybe I made mistakes! (*Crosses to* DAN) It is like my grandfather always said . . . We grow too soon old, and too late smart.
(*Pats* PETER *on shoulder.* PETER *and* KATIE *embrace.*)

RUTH

Dan, I think we'd better get going.

DAN

All right. Good-bye, Hilda.
(HILDA *is absorbed with young* AMISH MAN.)

RUTH

Leave her alone. She's working.

PAPA YODER

Mr. King, stay at least for the wedding.

DAN

We'd love to!

EMMA

(*Enters from house*)
Look at this! The wedding cake for Katie and Ezra!

HILDA

No, Emma! Katie and Peter!

EMMA

Katie and Peter!
(*Sings*)
This is all very new to me,
Knocks me right off my feet.

174

HILDA

(Sings)
Peter's getting her,
Papa's letting her.

ENSEMBLE

(Sings)
We got anyway plenty to eat!
(As HILDA *and* EMMA *proceed into the finale with the ensemble, wedding guests start to arrive with presents for* KATIE *and* PETER *while all sing "Plenty of Pennsylvania")*
Plenty of Pennsylvania!
You've never seen the likes of
Plenty of Pennsylvania—where anything grows!
Plenty of Pennsylvania!
No pastures green the likes of
Plenty of Pennsylvania—where anything grows!
All you need is some seed and a plow or two
And a bull who's keeping company with a cow or two.
Soon you've got
Plenty of Pennsylvania.
Sweet land of meadows golden
And fat red barns for holdin'
What goes to town on market day,
Plenty of anything—plenty of everything
In Pennsylvan-i-ay!

*(*RUTH *gives* KATIE *a red rose from her dress.* TWO YOUNG AMISH MEN *bring in a gaily painted dowry chest, on which* EMMA *places the wedding cake. An-*

other AMISH MAN *brings in an old-fashioned rocking chair.* THREE YOUNG AMISH LADIES *dance on with gaily colored Pennsylvania Dutch quilt.* TWO AMISH GIRLS *carry on a handsome tub. Another* AMISH GIRL *carries on a footstool to match the rocker. An* AMISH MAN *brings on a baby's cradle. And, as a climax to all the gifts,* DAN *hands* PETER *the deed to the River Farm. Everyone sings jubilantly and at the conclusion of "Plenty of Pennsylvania," the curtain falls.)*

Curtain

THE END